STIRRING IT UP, BLENDING IN, AND DROPPING BY
Recipes from your favorite West Cobb Realtors® & Staff

kw KELLERWILLIAMS® **REALTY**
SIGNATURE PARTNERS

AWARD
WINNING
RECIPES
&
MORE

SENSATIONAL

Cookbook

OVER 200 RECIPES

WE DO MORE THAN COOK UP SALES!

Sensational Cookbook
Published by Keller Williams Realty Signature Partners, Marietta GA

ISBN: 978-1519690326

Manufactured in the United States of America

Dedication

This cookbook is dedicated to the memory of Amanda Nicole Mitchell, beloved wife of Bruce Mitchell and mom of their two precious children, Morgan Alexandria Mitchell and Caleb Jude Mitchell.

Amanda was born in Rome, Georgia, May 3, 1980, daughter of Randy and Josie Hall. Amanda loved worshiping Jesus and living her life for the Lord. An amazing wife, mother, daughter, and sister, she cherished every moment spent with family. Known for her planning, she couldn't wait for vacation, especially if that included going to Disney World or Dollywood. Her care-free spirit shone through her arts and crafts, love of the outdoors, and avid running. She loved the Lord with all her heart, with all her soul, and with all her mind. Amanda left an amazing legacy of love in all of her family and friends. She will truly be missed as much as she was loved.

Amanda went to Heaven on Monday, October 19, 2015, surrounded by her loving family.

After expenses are covered, the proceeds of this book will be donated to a memorial fund for her children at United Community Bank, 7400 Adairsville Highway, Adairsville, GA 30103.

Acknowledgement

This cookbook was a collaborative project of the real estate agents, staff and families of Keller Wiliams Realty Signature Partners West Cobb. A special thank you to the "Committee" that put the cookbook together including Vickie Birchfield, Wendy Chambers, Diana Forgerson, Marna Friedman, Jessica Gillham, Nancy Hayes, Julie Stickler and Ellen Whitehead Naffziger.

And thank you to the agents that contributed recipes to create this cookbook ... Abby Hood, Alicia Tankersley, Beth Haigh, Bill Celler, Bonnie Mullinax, Callie Ruffus, Cecilia Nally, Cheryl Wheatley, Dana Schaefer, Deanna Morrell, Denise Hutchinson, Diana Forgerson, Dianne Piecuch, Fran Elrod, Gamalier Sturges, Heather Abramo, Jeff Buffo, Jeff VanHuss, Jenna Jackson, Jennifer Cowan, Jessica Gillham, Jill Van Nuis, Jo Cunningham, Joshua Chapman, Judson Reel, Karen Grattafiori, Kathy Bishop Vaughan, Katrice Edwards, Kelly Kramb, Kerry Barr, Kim Jeans, Kimberly Chaffins, Laura Miller Edwards, Leigh Ann Vega, Linda Miller, Lorraine Danielson, Lynn Doty, Mandi Bagwell, Marna Friedman, Mary Pierce, Melissa Gilbert, Michelle Queen, Millie Ann Morrell, Monique Csoke, Nancy Hayes, Natalia Armour, Patti Loveless, Pauline Hobbs, Priscilla Johnson, Prissy Dixon, Rachel Konieczny, Rebecca Singer, Renee Tiller, Rick Hale, Rosemarie Parrish, Sherri Levine, Tammy Amsler, Tammy Wissing, Teena Regan, Tom Wise, Trish Fox, Trish Levy, Valerie Davis, Vanessa Lohr, and Wendy Abney.

Table of Contents

Breakfast

Even if you don't make time for breakfast every day, these recipes are great for Sunday Brunch.

Bug's Blueberry Pancakes

This pancake recipe is Gluten Free.

Contributed by: Beth Haigh

Ingredients:

½ cup organic almond flour
½ cup organic coconut flour
1 T organic raw coconut palm sugar
1 t aluminum-free baking powder
¼ tsp Himalayan salt
2 tsp gluten-free vanilla extract
1 tsp organic almond extract
5 large pastured eggs
⅓ cup whole milk (coconut milk, almond milk and grass-fed raw cow's milk all work well)
2 Tbsp organic Grade B maple syrup
1 cup frozen blueberries (minus any liquid)
organic cold-pressed extra-virgin coconut oil or organic pastured butter

Directions:

1. Preheat griddle to 250°F or low.
2. By cooking them low and slow, the gentle proteins of the eggs are not as likely to be destroyed.
3. Add almond flour, coconut flour, coconut palm sugar, baking powder and salt to a bowl.
4. Stir to combine and break up any clumps.
5. In a second bowl, mix together vanilla, almond extract, eggs, milk and maple syrup.
6. Add wet ingredients to dry and mix batter gently.
7. Once combined, fold in frozen blueberries.
8. Heat small amount of coconut oil or butter on griddle.
9. Ladle batter onto slightly oiled griddle. (I use a muffin scoop.)
10. Let pancakes cook until bubbles form, loosen then flip.
11. Cook on second side until lightly browned.
12. Remove from griddle and place on cooling rack or serve. Yield: approx. 10 pancakes.

Note: We always make at least a double batch and put the extras on a cooling rack with a small pat of butter on each to soak into them then freeze between sheets of waxed paper or parchment paper in zipper baggies once cool. They make great snacks or grab-and-go breakfast food that is chocked full of protein, fiber and good fats to give energy and keep your family satiated.

Sausage Pancake Bites

Contributed by: Bonnie Mullinax

Directions:

1. Mix pancake mix as directed.
2. Add cooked sausage crumbles.
3. Spray mini muffin tin with Pam and fill with pancake batter.
4. Sprinkle the extra sausage on top.
5. Bake at 350 for 13 minutes or until golden brown.
6. Serve with butter and syrup.

Ingredients:

1 cup cooked sausage
1 box pancake batter

Breakfast Lasagna

This is a great "make-ahead prep" breakfast or brunch recipe.
I use frozen waffles and pancakes, you can use fresh
if you want to make them. Gather your favorite berries; I like blueberries/raspberries
and strawberries in this and then top with bananas.You can make it today,
cover it and put in the refrigerator till you are ready to cook it.

Contributed by: Judson Reel

Ingredients:

Pastry cream:
1½ teaspoons vanilla extract
6 egg yolks
1 ½ cups milk
¼ teaspoon salt
¼ cup all- purpose flour
¾ cup sugar
Frozen waffles & pancakes
Assortment of fresh or frozen berries (do not used canned).

Directions:

Make the Pastry Cream first.
1. In a 2 quart saucepan, combine sugar, flour, salt and milk and whisk; over medium heat, cook while stirring until mixture thickens.
2. In a small bowl with a fork, beat egg yolks slightly, beat small amount of milk mixture into yolks.
3. Slowly pour egg mixture back into milk mixture.
4. Stirring constantly, cook over medium low heat until mixture thickens.
5. Remove from heat and stir in vanilla extract.
6. Chill cream until ready to use.

Prepare Lasagna:
7. Get your casserole dish, spray with non-stick spray or put some butter on it, then dust with flour.
8. Then put down a layer of pastry cream, then waffles, pastry cream, then pancakes-- continue alternating those until your casserole dish is half full.
9. Spread out a layer of the berries you like, you can use fresh or frozen, do not use any canned fruit.
10. Finish layering just like you have been doing, waffles, pastry cream, pancakes till you get to the top edge.
11. You can make it today, cover it and put in the refrigerator till you are ready to cook it. Cook at 350 for 60 minutes .

Breakfast Casserole

Contributed by: Joshua Chapman

Directions:

1. Preheat oven to 350.
2. Combine sausage in skillet and brown.
3. Grease 9x13 inch pan.
4. Layer first 5 ingredients in pan.
5. Combine eggs, half & half, milk, soup and dry mustard and pour over other ingredients.
6. Bake for 90 minutes

Ingredients:

1 box seasoned Pepperidge Farms croutons (or any other brand)
2 cups shredded cheddar cheese
8 oz can sliced mushrooms, drained
1 lb mild sausage
1 lb hot sausage
6 eggs
1 pint half and half
1 cup milk
1 can cream mushroom soup
¾ teaspoon dry mustard

Christmas Morning Sweet Rolls

Contributed by: Laura Miller Edwards

Ingredients:

1 bag of Parker House Rolls
(24)
¾ cup pecans
1 stick butter
1 t. cinnamon
¾ cup brown sugar
regular sized box butter-
scotch pudding (not instant)

Directions:

1. Spray bundt pan w/cooking spray.
2. Layer ½ of the nuts on bottom, ½ rolls, sprinkle ½ of the pudding, repeat.
3. On stove, melt butter, cinnamon, & brown sugar.
4. Pour on top of rolls.
5. Cover w/towel and let rise overnight in a warm place.
6. In the morning, bake at 350 degrees for 25 minutes.
7. Put plate on top and flip.
8. Serve hot. Yum Yum!

Sour Cream Butter Biscuits

Contributed by: Denise Hutchinson

Directions:

1. Preheat oven to 400.
2. Mix flour and butter together, add sour cream and mix well.
3. Place a spoonful of batter into greased miniature muffin pans.
4. Bake 8 to 10 minutes or until golden brown.

Ingredients:

2 cups self-rising flour
2 sticks butter, softened
1 cup sour cream

Almond Banana Pancakes

Contributed by: Beth Haigh

Ingredients:

2 large, ripe organic bananas
2 large or extra-large pastured eggs
1 heaping tablespoon of raw creamy almond butter
blackberries and/or diced Granny Smith apple, for garnish, optional
organic pastured butter or cold-pressed organic coconut oil for griddle/skillet

Directions:

1. Mash the bananas, add the egg and mix well.
2. Stir in almond butter, adding more than a tablespoon if you want a more pancake-like texture.
3. Warm butter or coconut oil in a skillet or griddle on low.
4. Pour batter into small cakes.
5. Brown on each side and serve warm garnished with blackberries or apples.

French Toast Casserole

Contributed by: Jennifer Cowan

Directions:

1. Cut bread into 1-inch cubes (no crust- if Hawaiian bread just tear into pieces).
2. Put into large mixing bowl.
3. Whisk together remainder of wet ingredients.
4. Pour egg mixture over bread cubes & mix until well covered.
5. Pour into 9 x13 baking dish.
6. Cover with saran wrap and refrigerate overnight.
7. Next morning, Preheat oven to 350.
8. Melt butter and stir in brown sugar, nuts, and syrup.
9. Heat until all melted.
10. Pour over bread mixture and bake 40-45 minutes or until firm (set).
11. Let rest for 5 minutes before serving.

Ingredients:

1 large loaf French/ sourdough bread (if loaves are small use 2 loaves)- sliced and cubed (You can substitute the bread type- I like to use a large pkg. of Kings Hawaiian Bread from Costco- you can use 1 loaf)
5 eggs
1½ cups milk
1 cup Half and Half
1 ½ tsp vanilla
** I also add about 1 tsp cinnamon

TOPPING
½ c butter
1 c brown sugar
1 c chopped walnuts or pecans (optional)
3-4 T Pure Maple Syrup

Egg & Sausage Casserole

Contributed by: Judson Reel

Ingredients:

6 large eggs
2 cups milk
5-6 slices bread
½ tsp salt
1 lb sausage
1 cup grated cheddar
cheese

Directions:

1. Brown sausage, crumble and drain well.
2. Beat eggs - add cubed bread, milk and salt
3. Add cheese and sausage.
4. Pour into glass casserole dish (8 x 13)
5. Refrigerate or freeze until ready to bake.
6. Bake at 350 for 45 minutes (longer if frozen)

Best-Ever Grain Free Banana Bread

Contributed by: Katrice Edwards

Directions:

1. Preheat oven to 350
2. Combine all wet ingredients (use a food processor)
3. Then add in the rest of the ingredients
4. Pour batter into a well oil pan
5. Cook 60 minutes
6. Flip out of pan, slice and enjoy.

Ingredients:

4 ripe bananas - mashed two cups
4 eggs
½ cup of almond butter
4 tbls of butter earth balance
1 tablespoon cinnamon
¼ teaspoon of clove
½ cup of coconut flour
1teaspoon of baking soda
1 teaspoon of baking powder
1 teaspoon of vanilla
pinch of salt
cup of chocolate chips

Alabama Grits Casserole

Contributed by: Dianne Piecuch

Ingredients:

1 teaspoon salt
3 cups boiling water
¾ cup quick grits
½ pound Velveeta cheese - cubed
¾ stick melted butter
dash of tabasco
2 beaten eggs
1 pound sausage - cooked, drained, & crumbled

Directions:

1. Preheat oven to 325 degrees.
2. Bring 3 cups water to a boil.
3. Add 1 teaspoon salt.
4. Add grits & cook 5 minutes (covered).
5. Stir in cubed cheese and butter.
6. Mix well until cheese is melted.
7. Add eggs, sausage & dash of tabasco. Pour into oblong dish sprayed with no-stick cooking spray.
8. Cook at 325 degrees for 45 minutes.

Baked Grits

Contributed by: Mandi Bagwell

Directions:

1. Preheat oven to 350.
2. Bring water and salt to a boil.
3. Add grits to boiling water, stirring constantly for one minute.
4. Cover and cook, stirring occassionally, until grits are thick and creamy.
5. Temper eggs with a small amount of hot cooked grits, then add back to remaining grits.
6. Combine remaining ingredients with grits and pour into a 2-quart casserole dish.
7. Bake for 45 minutes.
8. Top with additional cheese, if desired, during last few minutes of baking.

Ingredients:

4 cups water
1½ tsp. salt
1 cup uncooked grits
2 eggs, beaten
8 Tbs (1 stick) butter
1½ cups grated Monterey Jack and Cheddar cheese (combined)
2 cloves garlic, crushed
Dash of cayenne pepper

Appetizers

They may be meant to be served before a meal, but some of these appetizers could be a meal alone!

Spicy Corn Dip

Contributed by: Kelly Kramb

Ingredients:

2 cans Mexican Corn
2 Cups Monterey Jack
  Cheese Shredded
1 Small Can Chopped
  Jalapenos Drained
1½ Cups Mayonnaise
1 Cup Parmesan Cheese

Directions:

1. Mix all ingredients together and pour into a baking dish
2. Place uncovered in a 350* oven about 30 minutes or until bubbly.
3. Remove and serve with tortilla chips.

YUMMY

Game Day Baked Spinach Dip

Contributed by: Marna Friedman

Directions:

1. Chop frozen spinach up fine in chopper/food processor and place in large bowl.
2. Drain artichoke hearts and chop up fine in chopper/food processor.
3. Mix all ingredients except parmesan cheese together in bowl.
4. Place mixture into oven safe serving bowl and proceed to step #5 or freeze until ready to serve.
5. Sprinkle with parmesan cheese and bake at 350 ° for 20-25 minutes or until browned; or place frozen dip in microwave until melted and then add parmesan cheese and place in broiler until cheese melts
6. Serve immediately.

Serve with sour cream and salsa, on a platter with tortilla chips and/or vegetables. Enjoy the game!

Ingredients:

12 oz. frozen chopped spinach
8 oz. shredded mozzarella cheese
8 oz. monterey jack cheese
⅓ C heavy cream
½ C sour cream
14.5 oz. can artichoke hearts, drained
4 oz. shredded parmesan cheese

Spinach Dip

Contributed by: Heather Abramo

Ingredients:

1 package (10 oz.) baby spinach, chopped or 1 pkg. (10 oz. frozen chopped spinach, thawed and squeezed dry.
1 container (16 oz) sour cream
1 cup Blue Plate Mayonnaise
1 package of vegetable recipe mix (I use Knorr)
1 can (8 oz) water chestnuts, drained and chopped
3 green onions chopped (I grated regular sweet onion about 3 T)

Directions:

1. Combine all ingredients.
2. Chill about 3 hours or overnight.

Guacamole

Contributed by: Natalia Armour

Directions:

1. Mash avocados with fork.
2. Add lemon juice, garlic, jalapenos, and tomato.
3. Mix together all ingredients.

Ingredients:

3 ripe avocados
1 lemon juiced
2 to 3 fresh garlic cloves
chopped finely
1 or ½ fresh jalapeno
chopped finely
1 large tomato chopped finely
(optional)

Rosalynn Carter's Cheese Ball

Contributed By: Laura Miller Edwards

Ingredients:

3 cups freshly grated sharp cheddar cheese
½ cup chopped pecans
½ small onion - finely grated
¼ cup mayonnaise (enough to moisten)
8 oz. jar strawberry jam

Directions:

1. Mix first 5 ingredients together and mold into a doughnut shape.
2. Refrigerate for a few hours. Just before serving put jam in the middle.
3. Garnish with chopped toasted pecans.
4. Serve with crackers or pretzel thins.

Hot Corn Dip

Contributed By: Denise Hutchinson

Directions:

1. Mix all ingredients together.
2. Bake in an 8 x 8 dish at 350 for appx 30 mins.

Ingredients:

1 can Fiesta/Mexican Corn (Drained)

1 small can RoTel (Not Drained)

1 8 oz block cream cheese (Room Temp)

8 oz sour cream

2 cups shredded Mexican cheese

Yummy Garlic
Tomato Bruschetta

Contributed By: Patti Loveless

Ingredients:

Loaf of fresh Italian Bread,
Sliced 1"+ thick
1 Cup Tomato, any kind,
chopped
Basil, chopped fine
½ Cup Red Onion, chopped fine
2 Garlic Cloves, chopped fine
2 Garlic Cloves, whole
1 T Olive Oil
2 tsp Butter
Salt, to taste
Black Pepper, to taste

Directions:

1. Preheat oven to 350°.
2. Melt butter and mix with olive oil.
3. Brush bread with oil mixture, place bread on a cookie sheet in a single layer and toast well.
4. Cut whole garlic cloves in half and rub each slice of bread thoroughly with the garlic.
5. Mix together the remaining ingredients.
6. Spread mixture over the bread and heat in the oven for 3 minutes.
7. Drizzle with remained of oil mixture.
8. Serve hot.

Baked Artichoke Spread

Contributed By: Diana Forgerson

Directions:

1. Preheat oven to 350.
2. In a large bowl, mix mayonnaise, parmesan, artichoke, mozzarella and garlic powder.
3. Transfer mix to 8x8 baking dish.
4. Bake 30 minutes or until the top is golden brown and bubbly.
5. Sprinkle with paprika and serve immediately on your favorite cracker or bread.
6. Because of the cheese, if this cools down it can be reheated in oven until the cheese is bubbly.

Ingredients:

2 cups shredded mozzarella cheese
1 cup mayonnaise
1½ tsp. garlic powder
1 cup grated Parmesan cheese
1 tsp. paprika
2 cans artichoke hearts, drained!

Onion Dip

Contributed By: Diana Forgerson

Ingredients:

I cup chopped sweet onion
1cup mayonnaise
2 cups grated Swiss cheese
2 cups Parmesan cheese

Directions:

1. Pour into baking dish.
2. Bake for 30 min. in 350 oven, or until lightly brown and bubbly on top.
3. Serve with crackers.

Buffalo Chicken Dip

Contributed By: Cheryl Wheatley

Directions:

1. Boil chicken and shred.
2. Mix ½ cup ranch and ½ cup red hot sauce and ½ cup cheese
3. Spread cream cheese on bottom of pan.
4. Add chicken to mix and pour in pan.
5. Cook at 350 for 20 minutes.
6. Add ½ cheese on top last 10 minutes in oven.

Ingredients:

1 package of chicken breasts

ranch dressing

2 8oz packages of soft cream cheese

red hot sauce

shredded cheese

Artichoke Dip

Contributed By: Jennifer Cowan

Ingredients:

3 8oz. bars of cream cheese softened
1 cup mayonnaise
1 cup grated Parmesan cheese
2 cloves minced garlic
3 cans artichoke hearts (in water- drained)
2-3 tablespoons chopped jalapenos

Directions:

1. Preheat oven to 350.
2. In large bowl combine cream cheese, mayonnaise, garlic, Parmesan cheese, jalapenos.
1. Mix together.
2. Chop artichokes and add to mixture.
3. Mix and pour dip into a 9x13 casserole dish.
4. Bake at 350 degrees for 35-45 minutes until bubbling and top is slightly browned.
5. Serve with Tostitos Scoops.

Mexican Dip

Contributed By: Lorraine Danielson

Directions:

1. Preheat oven to 350.
2. Mix all ingredients well in baking dish
3. Bake for 35 minutes until cheese is bubbly.

Serve with lime tortilla chips - yum!

Ingredients:

1 can Mexican corn (drain)
¾ cup mayonnaise
4 ounces diced jalapeños (drain)
1 jar pimento (4 oz) drain
1 cup Monterey jack cheese shredded (use Sargento since it is less oily)
½ cup Parmesan cheese shredded

Cajun Crackers

Contributed By: Jo Cunningham

Ingredients:

1 Box Saltine Crackers
2 cups Canola Oil
2 Packages (dry) Ranch Dressing Mix
1 Tablespoon Cayenne Pepper
1 Tablespoon Crushed Red Pepper

Directions:

1. Mix oil, ranch dressing mix and peppers in 2 gallon zip lock bag.
2. Add crackers and turn bag over and over to cover crackers with mixture.
3. Set bag on counter and turn every 20 minutes for 2 hours.
4. Place paper towels in bag to soak up extra oil (change out towels several times).

Buffalo Chicken Dip

Contributed By: Jeff Buffo

Directions:

1. Beat cream cheese and ranch dressing together for about 2 minutes until creamy.
2. Mix remaining ingredients together.
3. Top with Shredded Cheddar Cheese.
4. Bake (Uncovered) for 15-20 minutes at 350 Degrees.

Ingredients:

1 Package Large Cream Cheese

½ Cup Creamy Ranch Dressing

1 Large Can Pulled Chicken

½ Cup Texas Pete Buffalo Sauce

½ Package of Dry Ranch Dressing

Zesty Onion Dip

Contributed By: Sherri Levine

Ingredients:

2 T olive oil or 1 T oil and 1 T butter
1½ cups diced onions
¼ teaspoon kosher salt
1 cube beef bouillon
⅓ cup water
1½ cups sour cream
3/4 cup mayonnaise
2 t Worcestershire sauce, eyeball it
¼ teaspoon garlic powder
1 teaspoon ground thyme
¼ teaspoon ground white pepper
½ teaspoon kosher salt

Directions:

1. In a saute pan over medium heat add oil, heat and add onions and salt.
2. Cook the onions until they are caramelized, about 20 minutes.
3. Add bouillon cube to the pan with water and cook until it "melts" coats onions, stirring frequently, 3 minutes.
4. Remove from heat and set aside to cool.
5. Mix the rest of the ingredients, and then add the cooled onions.
6. Refrigerate and stir again before serving.

Pineapple Casserole

Contributed By: Deanna Morrell

Directions:

1. Preheat oven to 375 degrees.
2. Coat baking dish - I have done both in a 9X9 square pan and a 9X13 pan - just depends if you want it thin or thick.
3. Crush crackers and shred the cheese.
4. Combine flour, sugar, and cheese.
5. Stir in pineapple until evenly coated.
6. Place mixture evenly in dish; top with cracker crumbs.
7. Bake 25-30 min until golden and bubbly.

SO GOOD with ham!

Inzgredients:

Cooking spray
24 buttery-flavor crackers, crushed (RITZ work great)
7 oz white cheddar cheese shredded
6 TBSP all purpose flour
1 c sugar
2 (20 oz) cans of pineapple chunks in juice, drained

Crostini Appetizer

Contributed By: Deanna Morrell

Ingredients:

Sourdough bread or Baguettes
6 oz. soft cheese
Artichoke Hearts
6 oz. Blue Cheese
Dates or Fig Jam
6 oz, Brie
Cranberries
Apples

Directions:

1. Use thinly sliced sourdough or baguettes.
2. Cheese & artichoke hearts - Use 6 oz of a soft cheese of your choice with a pinch of salt. Spread cheese on baguette slices and broil until melted. Then top with marinated artichoke heart slice.
3. Blue Cheese with dates or fig jam - Top baguette slices with 6-8 oz of crumbles blue cheese. Top with chopped dates (6-8) or ¼-1/3 tsp of fig jam. Broil until cheese melts. Top with a drizzle of honey if desired.
4. Brie with cranberries & apples – Top baguette with small slices of Brie chop cranberries and apples and mix. Put fruit on brie & broil to melt cheese.

Vegetables

Vegetables can be side dishes or an entire meal. Check out some of our favorites.

Broccoli Casserole

Contributed by: Trish Levy

Ingredients:

2 6oz packages frozen broccoli or fresh broccoli florets
2 T butter or margarine
2 T all-purpose flour
1 t chicken flavored bouillon granules
¾ C milk
3 oz package cream cheese, softened
¼ t salt
4 green onions, sliced
1 C shredded cheddar cheese
Paprika

Directions:

1. Lightly butter 13x9x2 baking dish.
2. Place broccoli in dish and set aside.
3. Melt 2T butter in a heavy saucepan over low heat.
4. Add flour, stirring until smooth.
5. Cook 1 minute, stirring constantly.
6. Stir in bouillon.
7. Gradually add milk, cook over medium heat stirring constantly until thickened and bubbly.
8. Add cream cheese and salt stirring until smooth.
9. Stir in onion.
10. Spoon mixture over center of broccoli and sprinkle with cheese and paprika.
11. Cover with foil and bake at 350 for 20 min.
12. Remove foil and bake an additional 5-10 minutes.

Potato Casserole Supreme

Contributed by: Tammy Amsler

Directions:

1. Peel and boil potatoes until tender.
2. Drain and beat in a large bowl with electric mixer until fluffy, adding butter, seasonings and milk.
3. Check seasonings and add more salt if necessary.
4. Turn into a 9x13 casserole.
5. Fold cheese into whipped cream and spread over potatoes for topping.
6. Bake at 350° for about 25 minutes (only until golden brown).

This can be made ahead of time and topping added just before baking. Serves 8-10.

Ingredients:

8 medium baking potatoes
½ cup butter
2½ tsp. salt
¼ tsp. pepper
2/3 cup warm milk
1½ cups shredded cheddar cheese
1 cup (½ pint) heavy cream, whipped

Pecan Broccoli Casserole

Contributed by: Fran Elrod

Ingredients:

1 lb. fresh broccoli
1 can Cream of Mushroom soup
½ cup milk
¼ lb. grated cheddar cheese
1 cup chopped pecans
½ cup bread crumbs

Directions:

1. Cook broccoli in salted water until tender.
2. Drain and place in a greased 1 quart casserole dish.
3. Add cheese and pecans.
4. Mix soup and milk.
5. Pour over ingredients.
6. Top with bread crumbs and bake at 350 for 30 minutes.

Roasted Beets & Avocado

Contributed by: Beth Haigh

Directions:

1. Preheat oven to 375°F.
2. Loosely wrap the beets together in parchment paper or aluminum foil.
3. Roast beets until tender, approximately 30-45 minutes, depending on size.
4. Remove beets from oven and let cool for a few minutes.
5. Toss beets with avocado and season with salt.

Yield: 4 servings.
Note: We use red and golden beets. Can roast beets ahead of time.

Ingredients:

4 beets, scrubbed, trimmed, peeled, chopped (about 1" pieces)
1 large Haas avocado, peeled, pitted and chopped
Himalayan salt to taste

Squash Casserole

Contributed by: Nancy Hayes

Ingredients:

¼ cup olive oil
¼ to ½ yellow or vidalia onion
chopped up
4 large yellow squash,
cut in half lengthwise
and slice in 1/4" pieces
2 large zucchini, cut like the
yellow squash
2 cups heavy cream
12 ozs grated cheddar
4 c panko bread crumbs
Scant ½ tbsp salt
¼ tsp white pepper
1 sleeve of Ritz crackers,
crushed
1 cup fried onions (optional)

Directions:

1. In a very large skillet or stockpot over medium high heat, add oil.
2. Saute onion, squash and zucchini for 3-5 min.
3. Add cream and bring to a simmer.
4. Stir in the cheese, bread crumbs, salt and pepper.
5. Stir until cheese melts and mixture is combined.
6. Transfer mixture to a baking dish (9X12) or two smaller dishes. Freezes well at this point if wrapped airtight and put in the freezer.
7. Allow to thaw if cooking from frozen.
8. Sprinkle crushed crackers on top.
9. Bake 25-30 min at 350 degrees.
10. Garnish with fried onions if desired.

Takes about 15 min to prepare before baking. Makes a lot - serves 12.

Spinach with Raisins, Pine Nuts & Apples

Contributed By: Beth Haigh

Directions:

1. Wash and dry spinach.
2. Heat oil in sauté pan over medium heat.
3. Cook raisins, pine nuts, apple and shallots in oil about 5 minutes, stirring occasionally, until raisins are plump.
4. Stir in salt.
5. Gradually add spinach, tossing just until spinach is lightly wilted. Plate spinach mixture and sprinkle with lemon zest.
6. Serve immediately.

Ingredients:

2 large bunches or 20oz fresh organic spinach
2 T grapeseed oil
¼ cup organic unsulfured raisins
¼ cup pine nuts
¼ cup peeled and cubed organic Granny Smith apple
3-4 T diced shallots
1/4 tsp Himalayan salt
Ribbons of lemon zest for garnish

Sweet Potato Souffle

Contributed by: Priscilla Johnson

Ingredients:

3 cups peeled sweet potatoes (approx. 3 medium potatoes)
Pinch of Salt
1 cup sugar
½ cup light brown sugar
½ cup melted butter
2 eggs beaten separate first
1 tsp vanilla
⅓ cup Carnation Evaporated Can Milk
Touch of cinnamon

Directions:

1. Preheat oven to 350.
2. Place peeled potatoes in pot with just enough water to cover them and boil.
3. Once potatoes come to boil, boil for approx. 20 minutes.
4. Mash potatoes in mixing bowl until smoothed.
5. Use electric mixer to mix the potatoes to help rid of the strands. Repeat this 2-3 times until potatoes become nice and smooth.
6. Add half of the remaining ingredients to smooth potatoes and mix until blended.
7. Add remaining half of the above ingredients and continue to mix until blended smoothly.
8. Bake for 25-30 Minutes (can add marshmallows on top if preferred 5-minutes before removing).

Same Recipe makes for great Sweet Potato Pies (remember to brown crusts before adding souffle mix).

Butternut Squash Garlic Mashed Potatoes

Contributed By: Patti Loveless

Directions:

1. Cut potatoes into 1/2" squares, cover with water in pot and boil until soft.
2. Cut squash in half lengthwise, remove seeds, peel and cut into small squares.
3. Heat 1 T of butter in frying pan on medium.
4. Cook garlic and onion until onion is clear and soft.
5. Add squash and sauté until soft.
6. Add butter and let it melt.
7. Smash squash and fold into potatoes.
8. Stir in Half & Half until Potatoes are the consistency you desire. (Use more half & half if needed)
9. Salt and Pepper to taste. Serve hot.

Ingredients:

1 Medium Butternut Squash
5 Medium Red Potatoes
3 Cloves Garlic Minced
2 Cups Half and Half
½ Small Sweet Onion
Chopped 1 Stick Real Butter
Thyme
Salt & Pepper

Bacon Wrapped Roasted Asparagus

Contributed by: Patti Loveless

Ingredients:

Asparagus
Bacon (any kind you like...
pork works best)
Salt
Olive Oil
Pepper
Toothpicks

Directions:

1. Preheat oven to 400°.
2. Wrap Asparagus spears with bacon and secure with a toothpick.
3. Lay asparagus in a single layer on a baking sheet.
4. Salt and pepper asparagus, drizzle with olive oil.
5. Bake until bacon is completely cooked.
6. Asparagus will be soft and tasty.

Arroz Con Gandules

It's easy - give it a try

This is our Puerto Rican traditional Holiday rice dish. Gandules are also known as Pigeon Peas and can be found in Publix, and markets that cater to Latinos.

Contributed By: Gamalier Sturgis

Directions:

1. In a medium size caldero add the oil, tomato sauce, alcaparrado, sofrito and sazon.
2. Cook over medium heat for 4 minutes.
3. Add all other ingredients, and enough water to cover the rice 1" above the rice line.
4. Start with 1 teaspoon of salt stir and keep adding and mixing well until you are satisfied with the taste.
5. Bring to a boil and cook over high heat until most of the water is absorbed.
6. Once the water has been absorbed, stir gently from bottom to top - once or twice only, cover and turn the heat down to low.
7. Cook for 30 minutes or until the rice is tender.

Ingredients:

2 cups grain rice (rinsed)
4 to 5 cups of hot water, or beef broth
½ cup sofrito
16 ounce can of gandules
2 tablespoons of alcaparrado (cappers and olives mixed together)
1 packet of Sazon with achiote
1 can tomato sauce
3 tablespoons of oil
Salt & pepper to taste

Stirring the rice after it has begun cooking may cause it go get sticky or "amogollao." Any rice that sticks to the bottom of the pot is called "pegao" and is crispy and tasty and a favorite of all true Puerto Ricans. However, not everyone is skilled is making pegao - it is an art. To make great pegao make sure to use plenty of oil. Cook for about 10 minutes longer so the pegao gets crispy and keep your eye on it. Each time you cook rice - check to see how long it takes to make pegao just the way your family likes it. Finally - if you want a lot of pegao - use a bigger caldero which, of course, will have a larger bottom surface.

Easy Mexican Rice

Contributed by: Abby Hood

Ingredients:

1 cup thick 'n chunky salsa
2 cups uncooked rice
1 14.5 oz can chicken broth
1 cup water
3 Tbsp. butter or oil

Directions:

1. Melt butter in sauce pan.
2. Add rice and brown slightly.
3. Add chicken broth, salsa and water.
4. Bring to a boil.
5. Reduce heat to simmer and cook 20 minutes.

If using brown rice, make sure you use twice as much liquid as rice. Then cook on reduced heat for at least 45 to 50 minutes. I usually make this with white rice because I know it will turn out, but don't be afraid to experiment.

Cheesy Green Beans

Contributed By: Joshua Chapman

Directions:

1. Cook green beans with dill weed.
2. Drain then add dry mustard and cubed Velveeta.
3. Top with crumbled bacon.
4. Cook at 350 for 15 minutes.

Ingredients:

18 ounces frozen green beans
½ teaspoon dill weed
½ pound of Kraft Velveeta
1 teaspoon dry mustard
6 slices of bacon - cooked

Rosemary Potatoes

Contributed By: Kathy Bishop Vaughan

Ingredients:

New redskin potatoes, 6 – 8, sliced
2 T. extra virgin olive oil
1 T. chopped rosemary (fresh preferred)
1 T. minced garlic
1 t. thyme
½ t. white pepper
Dash or 2 of cayenne pepper
Salt to taste

Directions:

1. Mix oilve oil and spices.
2. Toss potatoes with mixture, and spread evenly in baking dish.
3. Bake at 350-400 degrees for 45 minutes, stirring occasionally. Broil the last 5 mins (but watch CLOSELY)

Sweet Potato Souffle

Contributed By: Tammy Wissing

Directions:

1. Beat sweet potatoes and other ingredients.
2. Pour into casserole dish and bake for about 20 minutes at 400.
3. Add marshmallows onto the top and bake for an additional 10 minutes at 350.

Ingredients:

3 big sweet potatoes
1¼ cup white sugar
2 eggs, well beaten
¾ stick butter, melted
½ tsp nutmeg
½ tsp cinnamon
1 bag miniature marshmallows

Squash Casserole

Contributed By: Patti Loveless

Ingredients:

2 cups Squash, cut into rounds
8 oz Sour Cream
½ cup Onions, chopped fine
2 cups Sharp Cheddar Cheese, grated
1 T minced Garlic
Ritz Crackers, 1 Long Package
2 Cups Chicken Stock
14 oz can Cream of Chicken Soup
Butter
Salt & Pepper

Directions:

1. Melt Butter in pan over medium heat.
2. Add onions and garlic.
3. Sautee' until onions are clear.
4. Add squash and chicken stock and heat to just boiling. Reduce heat to medium and cook until squash is soft and no stock is left.
5. Smash squash mixture.
6. In saucepan, heat sour cream, 1 cup of cheese, ½ package of
7. smashed crackers on low heat until cheese is melted.
8. Fold mixture into squash, salt and pepper to taste and pour into casserole dish.
9. Cover with remainder of cheese then crackers.
10. Place pats of butter on top of crackers.
11. Bake in over at 350° until crackers are golden brown.

Zucchini Boats

Contributed By: Beth Haigh

Directions:

1. Preheat oven to 300°F.
2. Slice zucchini in half lengthwise and cut off ends.
3. Using a spoon, scrape out seeds...will leave about ¼" of zucchini.
4. Place on parchment-lined baking sheet.
5. In skillet, brown meat with onion, garlic, salt and spices.
6. Move meat to a plate and cook mushrooms in meat juices/ fat.
7. Once mushrooms cooked and drained, add all back in to skillet; add olives and feta.
8. Stir to combine.
9. Spoon mixture into zucchini.
10. Bake for 10-15 minutes or until mixture begins to brown.

Note: Adapt quantities to your tastes. Can be changed up to do Italian-, Mexican-themed, etc. easily by adjusting add-ins. Campbell wants to make sure you know he helped craft this recipe.

Ingredients:

4 medium zucchini
1 lb ground meat (beef, chicken, turkey, lamb)
½ medium sweet onion, diced
2 cloves garlic, minced
salt and spices/herbs to taste (black pepper, cayenne pepper, and rosemary tastes great)
1 cup chopped mushrooms (cremini, Portobello and/or shiitake)
¼ cup pitted Kalamata olives, diced
½ cup sheep feta or unpasteurized/raw Parmigiano Reggiano

Potatoes O'Brien

Contributed By: Denise Hutchinson

Ingredients:

1 pkg. Ore-Ida O'Brien potatoes
1 small jar Cheez Whiz
1 small carton sour cream

Directions:

1. Butter a 9 x 11 inch baking dish and spread potatoes on bottom.
2. Sprinkle of pepper (optional).
3. Mix Cheez Whiz and sour cream until smooth; heat if necessary. (May need to add 2 to 3 tablespoons milk if too dry.)
4. Pour over potatoes and bake at 325 until bubbly in center and a little brown on top.

Gammy's Texas Corn

Contributed By: Kimberly Chaffins

Directions:

1. In a large cooking dish, mix the butter and cream cheese.
2. Stir in corn and desired amount of jalapenos.
3. Bake at 350° for 45 minutes stirring every 15 minutes.

Ingredients:

3 cans Shoepeg corn
(drain 2 cans)
1 stick butter, softened
8 oz. cream cheese, softened
¼ - ½ cup (or more) jalapenos,
chopped – (canned - not
pickled)

Carrot Souffle

Contributed By: Wendy Abney

Ingredients:

1 (16oz) pkg baby carrots
3 large eggs
½ - ¾ cup sugar
½ cup light sour cream
¼ cup butter, softened
¼ cup all-purpose flour
1 ½ tsp baking powder
¼ tsp cinnamon

Directions:

1. Cook carrots in boiling water to cover in a large saucepan until tender.
2. Drain well; cool.
3. Process carrots and eggs in a food processor until smooth, stopping to scrape down sides.
4. Add sugar and remaining ingredients; process 30 seconds or until smooth.
5. Pour into lightly greased 8-in square baking dish.
6. Bake at 350 for 55-60 min. or until set.

Vegetable Casserole

Contributed By: Jo Cunningham

Directions:

1. Mix all vegetables, soup, etc together and put in a 9 x 13 baking dish.
2. Cover with crushed Ritz crackers and remaining butter.
3. Bake @ 350 for 30-45 minutes.

Ingredients:

3 cans Veg-All, drained well
1 cup mayonnaise
1 can Cream of Chicken soup
½ stick melted butter
1 can water chestnuts, drained
& chopped salt & pepper to taste
1 large onion chopped

TOPPING:
½ c Ritz crackers, crushed
1 stick melted butter

Baked Corn

Contributed By: Jo Cunningham

Ingredients:

1 cup milk
2 Tbsp butter
1 Tbsp Sugar
2 Tbsp Flour
1 15 oz can whole corn (drained)
2 eggs (well beaten)

Directions:

1. Boil ¾ cup milk with butter and sugar.
2. Dissolve flour in ¼ cup milk.
3. Pour flour mixture into milk mixture to make a thin white sauce.
4. Add to drained corn and mix in eggs.
5. Pour into a 1 to 1.5 quart Pyrex loaf pan.
6. Bake 1 hour at 400 degrees.

Cafeteria Carrot Souffle

Contributed By: Jo Cunningham

Directions:

1. Boil carrots in large pot of salted water until tender (about 15 minutes).
2. Drain and mash.
3. Mix melted butter, white sugar, flour, baking powder with mashed carrots.
4. Add vanilla extract and eggs.
5. Mix well and transfer to a 2 quart casserole dish.
6. Sprinkle with confectioner sugar.
7. Bake at 350 degrees for 30 minutes

Ingredients:

2 pounds carrots (chopped)
½ cup melted butter
1 cup white sugar
3 tablespoons all-purpose flour
1 teaspoon baking powder
1 teaspoon vanilla extract
3 eggs beaten
1 teaspoon confectioner sugar for dusting

Sweet Potato Casserole with Pineapple Topping

Contributed By: Jo Cunningham

Ingredients:

½ Stick of Butter
2 Cups Mashed Sweet Potatoes
¼ Cup Milk
2 Eggs
1 Tsp. Vanilla
1 cup Sugar

TOPPING:
1 - 8 oz. can crushed pineapple (drained)
¼ cup flour
½ cup sugar
1 egg
1 stick melted butter

Directions:

1. Mash boiled sweet potatoes, melt butter and combine with milk, eggs, sugar and vanilla.
2. Pour into 9x9 baking dish.
3. Combine all topping ingredients and spread over top of potato mixture.
4. Bake at 350 degrees for 30 minutes.

NOTE: Recipe can be doubled and baked in a 9x13 dish.

Drunken Cranberries

Contributed By: Deanna Morrell

Directions:

1. Preheat oven at 275 degrees.
2. Put cranberries, sugar, orange pieces, orange zest and water into ovenproof skillet.
3. Bake 1 hour.
4. Take out and stir.
5. Put back into oven for 1 hour.
6. Take out again, and stir.
7. Add Brandy.
8. Put back into oven for 45 minutes.
9. Remove from oven, stir in ⅓ cup of Brandy.
10. Let completely cool.
11. Store in airtight containers. (Suggestion: put into several smaller containers to use several times).

Ingredients:

1 cup of water (add if needed to cover berries)
2 bags of fresh cranberries
1 cup of sugar
2 oranges chopped into small pieces
2 tbsp fresh orange zest
1 cup of brandy & ⅓ cup

Southern Style Green Beans

Contributed By: Teena Regan

Ingredients:

2 bags of frozen Italian Cut Beans
1 Salt Pork
1 can of coke

Directions:

1. Slow boil greens with salt pork for 3 hours.
2. Put in crockpot with remaining water and add one can of coke.
3. Slow simmer for 4 hours.

Squash Casserole

Contributed By: Rachel Konieczny

Directions:

1. Put well drained hot squash in large mixing bowl.
2. Add beaten egg, mayonnaise, butter, sugar, half of cheese and half of Ritz crackers crumbs.
3. Mix well and season with salt and pepper to taste.
4. Put in a buttered 1.5-quart baking dish.
5. Top casserole with remaining half of cheese and half Ritz cracker crumbs.
6. Bake @ 350 degrees for twenty minutes.

Ingredients:

2-3 cups cooked squash
1 egg (beaten)
½ cup mayonnaise
1 ½ cup of Ritz cracker crumbs (divided)
½ stick of butter sliced, plus extra to butter baking dish
1 tablespoon sugar
1 cup grated cheddar cheese (divided)
Salt & Pepper to taste

Barb's Mushrooms

Contributed By: Vanessa Lohr

Ingredients:

2 lb. Mushrooms (washed thoroughly)
1 stick melted margarine
1 pinch of salt
½ tsp pepper
1 tsp garlic powder
1 tsp lemon juice
1 tbsp. beer
2 tbsp. Worcestershire Sauce

Directions:

1. Prepare mushrooms by slicing off the bottom of the stems and wash thoroughly (wash mushrooms individually for best results). Cut larger mushrooms in half.
2. In large skillet, melt margarine and add just enough water to barely cover the bottom.
3. Add next five ingredients and bring to a slow bubble (medium heat).
4. Stir in mushrooms and coat each thoroughly.
5. Sprinkle Worcestershire sauce over mushrooms enough to coat (amount may vary).
6. Stir and bring to boil.
7. Cover and simmer on VERY LOW until done (45 minutes to 1 hour) checking every 15 minutes.
8. Add more seasoning to taste.

Sweet Potato Casserole

Contributed By: Nancy Hayes

Directions:

1. Boil and mash potatoes.
2. Mix in sugar, butter, eggs, vanilla, and milk.
3. Put in a 13x9 baking dish.
4. For topping, melt the butter and mix in the other ingredients.
5. Sprinkle on top of the potato mixture.
6. Bake 25 min at 350 degrees.

Got this recipe from Christy Medford who used to work here - it is easy peesy and SO good!

Ingredients:

3 c sweet potatoes, peeled and cut into pieces (about 4 good sized ones)
½ c sugar
½ c butter
2 eggs, beaten
1 tsp vanilla
⅓ c milk

Topping:
⅓ c melted butter
1 c light brown sugar
½ c flour
1 c chopped pecans

Breads

Homemade bread can compliment any meal, or just enjoy a slice by itself!

World Famous VanHuss Corn Bread

Contributed by: Jeff VanHuss

Ingredients:

1⅓ Self-rising corn meal
⅓ Cup Self-rising flour
2 Tablespoons Sugar
1 Cup Buttermilk (or 1 cup milk with 1 tsp. vinegar)
1 Egg

Directions:

1. Preheat oven to 425 degrees.
2. Prepare 8 inch cast iron skillet with 2 tbsp. canola oil and 2 tbsp. butter - place skillet in over to preheat.
3. Mix dry ingredients.
4. Mix buttermilk and egg and add to dry ingredients.
5. Mix well and add to preheated skillet.
6. Bake 20 minutes at 425 degree - serve hot with butter!

Sour Cream Butter Biscuits

Contributed by: Denise Hutchinson

Directions:

1. Preheat oven to 400.
2. Mix flour and butter together, add sour cream and mix well.
3. Place a spoonful of better into greased miniature muffin pans.
4. Bake 8 to 10 minutes or until golden brown.

Ingredients:

2 cups self-rising flour
2 sticks butter, softened
1 cup sour cream

My Mama's Yeast Rolls

Contributed by: Nancy Hayes

Ingredients:

1 c shortening (crisco - NOT butter flavored)
1 c sugar
1½ tsp salt
1 c boiling water
2 beaten eggs
2 pk regular dry yeast
1 c. lukewarm water
6 c. plain unsifted flour

Directions:

1. Place the shortening, sugar, and salt in the bottom of a very large bowl because you will be using this bowl to mix the rolls (and to let the dough rise in).
2. Pour boiling water over these ingredients - blend (with mixer) and allow to cool. It won't be a completely smooth mixture - it's okay to have tiny clumps in it.
3. While it's cooling, put 1 cup of lukewarm water in a 2 (or more) cup measure.
4. Add the yeast and stir until dissolved.
5. Add the beaten eggs and water with yeast to the shortening mixture. Combine.
6. Then add the flour a little at a time.
7. Mix well in between additions of flour - I usually put in about a third of it at a time. The more flour that goes in, the harder it is to mix. Be patient and keep pushing mixture down off the mixing paddles.
8. Once it is fully combined, cover the bowl tightly with saran wrap and put in the refrigerator for at least 4 hours so it can rise. I usually leave it overnight.*
9. About 3 hours before baking, prepare 3 large sheet pans by coating them with butter or cooking spray (butter works the best!).
10. Cover your counter or wherever you want to roll out the dough with just enough flour so that the dough won't stick.
11. Roll out the dough pretty thin.
12. I use a circular cutter to cut the biscuits. When I place them on the pan, I pick up one side of the circle and press it over the other side slightly. This makes a very pretty roll (and it's

what Mama did!). Don't put them too close together.

13. I usually roll out a third of the dough at a time and the recipe will fill 3 large baking sheets.
14. The rolls will rise at room temp over the next 3 hours.
15. Bake at 425 degrees for 12-15 min.
16. Keep a close eye on them and don't let them burn. Immediately when you remove a pan from the oven, use a stick of butter and rub some over the top of each roll so that it melts into it - yummy!

*You can make the dough way ahead of time. It keeps 7-10 days in the fridge before you roll them out to bake. (Do NOT put the dough in the freezer!)

Growing up, these yeast rolls were the star of any holiday get-together we had. Probably a full pan of them got eaten before we ever even sat down to dinner! After my mama died, my sisters tried their hand at these rolls and both said they just couldn't get it right. My first couple of attempts didn't turn out so great but since then, I have become the yeast roll maker for the family. Every time I'm in my kitchen rolling them out, I clearly see my mama doing the same thing for us so many times during my life. So if your first try at these isn't successful, don't give up! Please try them again because when you get it right, the finished rolls can't be beat!

Best-Ever Grain Free Banana Bread

Contributed by: Katrice Edwards

Ingredients:

4 ripe bananas - mashed two
cups
4 eggs
½ cup of almond butter
4 T butter earth balance
1 tablespoon cinnamon
¼ teaspoon of clove
½ cup of coconut flour
teaspoon of baking soda
teaspoon of baking powder
teaspoon of vanilla
pinch of salt
cup of chocolate chips

Directions:

1. Preheat oven to 350.
2. Combine all wet ingredients (use a food processor).
3. Then add in the rest of the ingredients.
4. Pour batter into a well oil pan.
5. Cook 60 minutes.
6. Flip out of pan, slice and enjoy.

Salad

Sometimes it's served before a meal, sometimes after, but then sometimes it's a meal in itself!

Apple Fruit Salad

Contributed by: Fran Elrod

Ingredients:

1 8 oz, package cream cheese
¾ cup sugar
1 small can crushed pineapple
1 diced apple
1 cup pecans
1½ cups small marshmallows
1 jar cherries, drained
10 oz. Cool Whip

Directions:

1. Soften cream cheese.
2. Blend cream cheese and sugar.
3. Fold in the rest of the ingredients and chill.

Chef Aaron's Chicken Salad

Contributed by: Vanessa Lohr

Directions:

Mix all Ingredients well - this Chicken Salad stores well in an airtight container.

Ingredients:

4 cups diced cooked chicken
(Roasted Chicken is great)
1 cup diced celery
¾ cup - Craisins
(Dried cranberries)
¾ cup Slivered Almonds
½ cup small Diced Onion
¾ cup mayonnaise - (add
enough to not be dry)
Salt & Pepper

Summer Cabbage Slaw Salad

Contributed by: Bonnie Mullinax

Ingredients:

4 cups cabbage slaw (pre-chopped, I love Trader Joe's) or 1 head green cabbage finely chopped
1 bell pepper, any color, chopped
1 avocado, cubed
1 ear organic corn, kernels sliced off the cob
1 can pinto beans, rinsed and drained
1 organic chicken breast OR 6 thin cut chicken tenders OR 1 medium piece wild fish OR 8 wild prawns to grill
a few cilantro leaves to garnish

Directions:

Make Honey Cilantro Hot Sauce Dressing (next page) first by combining all ingredients in a blender. Set aside.

1. Grill chicken, fish or shrimp of your choice on the stovetop or BBQ over high heat, flipping only when you get a good sear on the first side.
2. Slice or keep whole to serve.
3. Add cabbage, pinto beans, corn, peppers and avocado to a large bowl.
4. Toss salad with dressing.
5. Add grilled chicken, fish or shrimp over the top and sprinkle with extra cilantro to garnish.

Honey Cilantro Hot Sauce Dressing

Contributed by: Bonnie Mullinax

Directions:

1. Combine all ingredients in a blender.
2. Set aside.

Ingredients:

4 T olive oil
2 T whole milk Greek yogurt
3 tsp honey
2 tsp hot sauce (or more if you like spicy things)
½ cup cilantro leaves
Juice from 1 ripe lime (1 large or 2 small)
¼ tsp sea salt + ½ tsp pepper

Slaw Made For A Dog

Contributed By: Patti Loveless

Ingredients:

1 medium head of cabbage
Mayonnaise
Salt & Pepper

Directions:

1. Quarter cabbage, place in large bowl and cover with water.
2. Let cabbage soak to clean.
3. Rinse cabbage and let water drain.
4. Cut stalk out of cabbage quarters.
5. Using a grinder or grater, grind or grate cabbage (pieces should be small).
6. Mix in mayonnaise to desired consistency (best if very moist), salt and pepper to taste.
7. Let slaw set in the refrigerator, overnight if possible.
8. Stir well.
9. Cover your favorite hot dog and enjoy.

Southern Potato Salad

Contributed by: Patti Loveless

Directions:

1. Cut potatoes into small squares.
2. Place potatoes in large pot and just cover with water, boil until almost done but still firm.
3. Let potatoes cool completely.
4. Finely chop 3 of the hard boiled eggs, reserving the 4th egg.
5. Place cooled potatoes in a large bowl, fold in pickles and mustard.
6. Fold in mayonnaise until salad is very moist.
7. Fold in salt and Pepper.
8. Cut reserved egg into thin rounds and place on top of the salad.
9. Sprinkle with smoked paprika.
10. Cover and let salad set in refrigerator. Serve chilled.

Note: Do not overcook potatoes. Fold ingredients into potatoes to prevent mashing potatoes up.

Ingredients:

4-5 Medium Red Potatoes, Peeled
¼ Cup Yellow Mustard
4 Eggs, Hard Boiled & Peeled
¼ Cup Sweet Pickles, Chopped fine
¼ Cup Sour Pickles, Chopped fine
Mayonnaise
Salt & Pepper
Smoked Paprika

Broccoli Salad

Contributed By: Joshua Chapman

Ingredients:

1½ lbs. of ground beef
1 T of vegetable oil
1 large onion 1 large bag (32 oz) broccoli
1 lb sliced mushrooms
3 finely chopped green onions

Marinade
1½ cups canola oil
⅓ cup cider vinegar plus a splash more (if doubling use ¾ cup)
¾ cup sugar
1½ tsp salt
1½ tsp paprika
1½ tsp celery seed
1½ tsp. onion powder

Directions:

1. Mix marinade pour over vegetables.
2. Marinate at least 3 hours.
3. Stir several times while marinating to redistribute the marinade.
4. Drain before serving.

Zesty Summer Cole Slaw

Contributed By: Jenna Jackson

Directions:

1. In partially covered microwave-safe bowl, microwave golden raisins and lime juice 20 seconds.
2. In separate bowl, whisk together olive oil, mustard, garlic and thyme.
3. Season with salt, if desired.
4. Add coleslaw mix, radishes, carrots, scallions and raisins; toss.
5. Garnish with lime slices, if desired.

Ingredients:

½ cup golden raisins

1 Tbs. lime juice

⅓ cup olive oil

2 Tbs. Dijon mustard

1 tsp. chopped garlic

½ tsp. dried thyme

1 bag (16 oz) coleslaw mix

½ cup radishes, julienned

½ cup shredded carrots

2 scallions, chopped

Famous Chicken Salad

Contributed By: Rachel Konieczny

Ingredients:

4 chicken breast, boiled, deboned, shredded
2-3 bay leaves
3 cubes chicken bouillon
1 to 2 cups toasted pecans
1 – 1½ cups chopped celery
Mayonnaise to bind
2 tsp Cavender's Greek Seasoning
Salt & Pepper to taste

Directions:

1. Place chicken, bay leaves and bouillon in a pot with enough water to bring to a boil, lower to medium heat until done (about an hour).
2. Debone and shred chicken.
3. Combine chicken with remaining ingredients and chill.
4. Great for summer picnics!

Claremont Salad

Contributed By: Marna Friedman

Directions:

1. Place the vegetables together in a large mixing bowl.
2. Shake the sugar, vinegar, salad oil, water, and salt together in a large jar and pour the mixture over the vegetables.
3. Leave the vegetables and mix at room temperature for two (2) hours.
4. Put it in the refrigerator overnight to marinate.
5. Done, enjoy !!

Ingredients:

2 tablespoons sugar
3 tablespoons vinegar
2 tablespoons of salad oil
1 tablespoon of water
1 teaspoon of salt
2 cucumbers (diced)
1 carrot (diced)
1 green pepper (diced)
1 bermuda onion (sliced)
1 head of cabbage (shredded)

Best Ever Cole Slaw

Contributed By: Karen Grattafiori

Ingredients:

8 oz. cabbage, shredded or mix
3-4 green onions, sliced
1 package chicken flavor
Ramen noodles, broken into
pieces
½ cup slivered almonds
2 Tbsp. sesame seeds

Dressing:
2 Tbsp. sugar
3 Tbsp. vinegar
½ tsp. salt
½ tsp. pepper
½ cup oil
Flavoring packet from noodles

Directions:

1. Toast almonds and sesame seeds at 300° for 8-10 minutes being careful not to burn.
2. Combine cabbage, green onions and chicken flavor.
3. Mix dressing ingredients together.
4. Pour dressing over cabbage mixture and stir.
5. Mix almonds and seeds with slaw mixture right before serving.

Grape Salad

Contributed By: Kimberly Chaffins

Directions:

1. In a large bowl, mix cream cheese, sour cream, brown sugar, and vanilla until blended.
2. Fold in grapes.
3. Sprinkle with pecans to completely cover.
4. Cover and refrigerate until serving.

Ingredients:

8 oz. cream cheese, softened
5 oz. sour cream
1 cup brown sugar
2 tsp. vanilla
2 lbs. seedless red grapes
(small in size if available)
2 cups chopped pecans

Broccoli Salad

Contributed By: Millie Ann Morrell

Ingredients:

1 bag fresh broccoli
½ cup chopped red onion
¾ cup cashew pieces
¾ cup raisins
5 pieces of bacon (cooked and crumbled)
1½ cup coleslaw dressing (I used Marzetti's)
handful of shredded cheese

Directions:

1. Combine and mix all but cheese.
2. Sprinkle cheese on top
3. Refrigerate for a couple of hours for flavors to combine

Soups

Imagine relaxing on a cold evening with a nice hot, bowl of soup.
Here are some great options.

Barley Beef & Veggie Soup

Contributed by: Lynn Doty

Ingredients:

1 cup barley
2 T. extra virgin olive oil
3 cloves pressed garlic
1 small sweet onion – chopped
1 small steak (filet)
½ cup red wine
½ cup yellow peppers
½ cup red baby peppers
1 cup chopped carrots
1 cup diced celery
1 cup chopped kale
1 15 oz. can of diced tomatoes
3 cups of organic beef broth

Directions:

1. Place barley in 2½ cups of water and bring to a boil.
2. Turn down and cook on low for 45 minutes.
3. In the meantime, sauté garlic and chopped onion extra virgin olive oil in large sauté pan (big enough for filet and vegetables to be added later).
4. Add chopped filet.
5. Sauté chopped filet until it is browned a bit.
6. Add red wine and let it bubble a little.
7. Place in a large stockpot and add chopped vegetables, can of diced tomatoes and 3 cups of organic beef broth.
8. Turn down the heat and let it "get to know itself" for about 1 hour.
9. Add the cooked barley and ½ - 1 teaspoon ground Chipotle Pepper, ¼ cup chopped cilantro, dash each of sea salt and fresh ground pepper.
10. Enjoy!

Tom Kha Gai

Thai Coconut Chicken Soup

Contributed by: Beth Haigh

Directions:

1. Combine the broth/stock, Kaffir lime leaves, lemongrass, galangal, fish sauce, lime juice and chilies and bring to a boil.
2. Reduce to a simmer and let cook for about an hour to allow the flavors to meld.
3. Add in sriracha, mushrooms and coconut milk and return to a simmer.
4. Add in chicken and simmer until chicken is cooked through - usually about 5 minutes.

Note: Use organic ingredients whenever possible. Galangal and Kaffir lime leaves can be found in the produce section of Asian markets (local or Super H Mart) or Amazon, if you can't find in your local grocery store. Please check ingredients for the fish sauce: should contain ONLY fish, water, salt.

Ingredients:

4 C (32oz) organic chicken broth

3 Kaffir lime leaves, torn

3 2" pieces of fresh lemongrass, bruised to help release flavor

3 1" pieces of fresh galangal, peeled

2 Tbsp fish sauce

2 T. freshly-squeezed lime juice

2 Thai chili peppers, sliced in half

1 Thai Bird's Eye chili, sliced in half (optional)

1 tsp Sky Valley by Organicville Sriracha

2 cups sliced shiitake mushrooms

2 (16oz) cans whole coconut milk

2 lbs chicken breasts, thinly sliced

2-3 Tbsp cilantro or chives, chopped (optional for garnish)

"Copy Cat" LaParrilla Chicken Soup

No Kidding- This soup tastes just like the Chicken Tortilla Soup
at our favorite Mexican restaurant!

Contributed by: Vanessa Lohr

Ingredients:

2 Tbsp olive oil
1 medium yellow onion
2 stalks celery
1 medium jalapeno
4 cloves garlic
¾ lb. chicken breast
6 cups chicken broth
1 (14.5 oz.) can diced
tomatoes w/chiles
1 tsp oregano
½ Tbsp cumin
½ bunch cilantro
1 medium avocado

Directions:

1. Dice the onion, celery, and jalapeno (scrape the seeds out of the jalapeno before dicing).
2. Mince the garlic.
3. Cook the onion, celery, jalapeno, and garlic in olive oil over medium heat for about 5 minutes or until tender.
4. Add the chicken breast, chicken broth, canned tomatoes with chiles, oregano, and cumin to the pot.
5. Bring the whole pot up to a boil over high heat then reduce the heat to low, place a lid on top, and let simmer for one hour.
6. After simmering for an hour with a lid on, carefully remove the chicken breast from the pot and use two forks to shred the meat.
7. Return the meat to the pot.
8. Squeeze the juice of one lime into the soup. Get as much juice as possible from the lime by using a spoon to scrape the inside of the lime.
9. Rinse the cilantro and then roughly chop the leaves.
10. Add to the pot, give it a quick stir, and serve.
11. Dice the avocado and add a few chunks to each bowl.

New England Corn Chowder

Contributed by: Fran Elrod

Directions:

1. Cook celery, onion, and bacon in 6-8 quart Dutch oven over medium heat for 10-15 minutes or until vegetables are tender.
2. Stir occasionally.
3. Add corns, milk, stock, cream and bottled hot sauce.
4. Bring to boiling and then reduce heat.
5. Simmer covered for 30 minutes.
6. Add potatoes.
7. Return to boiling.
8. Reduce heat.
9. Simmer covered for about 15 minutes or more until potatoes are tender.
10. While the soup is simmering, stir together the butter and flour in a small bowl until smooth.
11. Add the flour mixture to corn mixture.
12. Cook and stir until thickened and bubbly.
13. Cook and stir 1 minute more.

Ingredients:

1 cup chopped celery (2 stalks)
½ cup chopped onion
2 slices bacon, chopped
2 (15 oz.) cans whole kernel corn, drained
2 (15 oz.) cans cream style corn
4 cups milk
3½ cups chicken or turkey stock or 2 (14 oz.) cans reduced sodium chicken broth
1 cup whipping cream
3-4 dashes of bottled hot pepper sauce
4 cups cubed potatoes
¼ cup butter, softened
¼ cup all-purpose flour
Salt and pepper

Chicken & Sausage Gumbo Soup

Contributed by: Vanessa Lohr

Ingredients:

2 pounds Andouille
Sausage (Mild or Hot)
4 large chicken breast
1 bag frozen okra
2 large (32 oz) Chicken
Broth
1 large onion - diced
1 green pepper - diced
Salt - Pepper and Cajun
spice to taste

Directions:

1. Brown Andouille Sausage in a skillet- transfer to large stock pot
2. Rub Chicken with Cajun spices or Ground red pepper (control the heat by the kind of pepper you use)
3. Cook Chicken breast in skillet with the diced onions and pepper - add to pot
4. Add Broth
5. Bring to a boil - turn down to simmer about 1 hour - add okra and simmer 30 min longer.

This is like gumbo without the flour- a great winter soup!

Black Bean & Sausage Posole

Contributed By: Tom Wise

Directions:

1. In a large saucepan, brown sausage.
2. Drain off fat.
3. Stir in broth, black beans, hominy, tomatoes, potatoes, green pepper, onion, garlic, chili powder, and oregano.
4. Bring to boil, reduce heat.
5. Cover and simmer for 30 minutes.

Ingredients:

1 12-oz. package turkey & pork sausage

2 14 ½-oz. cans chicken broth

1 15-oz. can black beans, rinsed & drained

1 14 ½ -oz. can golden hominy, rinsed & drained

1 14 ½ -oz. can Mexican-style stewed tomatoes

1 cup diced hash browns, frozen

½ cup green pepper, chopped

1/3 cup onion, chopped

1 clove garlic

½ teaspoon chili powder

1 teaspoon oregano, dried, crushed

Ham & Corn Chowder

Contributed By: Jenna Jackson

Ingredients:

2 Tbsp butter
½ cup chopped onion
1 cup chopped red and green bell peppers
1 cup diced ham
1 can cream of mushroom soup
1 can cream style corn
1 cup diced potatoes (canned is fine)
1 cup whole milk
½ cup heavy cream
Salt & pepper and Cajun seasoning

Directions:

1. Saute ham in butter… add onions and peppers.
2. Cook until tender.
3. Blend in soup, then milk and cream.
4. Add corn, potatoes and seasoning.
5. Simmer and serve.

Cream of Potato Soup

Contributed By: Cecilia Nally

Directions:

1. Saute onion in margarine in large saucepan until onion is tender.
2. Add potatoes, hot water, bouillon cubes, salt and white pepper.
3. Simmer until potatoes are tender.
4. Mash slightly.
5. Add milk and half & half.
6. Cook over low heat until heated through; do not boil.
7. Add Cheese, stirring until melted.

Ingredients:

1 cup finely chopped onion
½ cup margarine
3 cups cubed peeled potatoes
1 cup hot water
2 chicken bouillon cubes
2 tsps salt
¼ tsp white pepper
3 cups milk
½ cup half and half
2 cups shredded sharp cheddar cheese.

Chicken Tortilla Soup

Contributed By: Cecilia Nally

Ingredients:
1 - 16 oz can of corn, drained
(whole kernel)
1 - 16 oz cans black beans
1 - 16 oz can northern beans
2 - 16 oz cans rotel tomatoes
⅓ cup salsa (if I have it
available I like to use Tostidos
Party Powl Southwestern Salsa)
3 cups chicken broth
2 cups chopped cooked
chicken
2 tespoons cumin
Corn or flour tortillas, cut into
small pieces
1 cup shredded Moterey Jack
or Cheddar Cheese

Directions:
1. Combine corn, undrained beans, tomatoes, salsa, broth, chicken, and cumin in a large sauce pan.
2. Simmer for 30 minutes to blend flavors, stirring from time to time.
3. Serve topped with tortilla pieces and cheese.

Karen's Chicken Tortilla Soup

Contributed By: Karen Grattafiori

Directions:

1. Combine all ingredients except chips and cheese in a large slow cooker.
2. Cover and cook on low 8 hours.
3. Just before serving, remove chicken and pull with two forks or slice into bite-sized pieces.
4. Stir back into soup.
5. To serve, put a handful of chips in each bowl.
6. Ladle soup over chips and top with cheese.

Ingredients:

4 chicken breast halves
2-15 oz. cans black beans, not drained
2-15 oz. cans Rotel tomatoes
1 cup salsa
4 oz. can chopped green chilies
14.5 oz. can tomato sauce
1-2 cans corn, drained
1 can chicken broth
Tortilla chips
Grated cheddar cheese

Corn Chowder

Contributed By: Kathy Bishop Vaughn

Ingredients:

2 T. butter
¾ cup onions, chopped
½ cup celery, chopped
1 sweet red pepper, minced
4 cups fresh sweet corn
(canned or frozen is fine)
½ t. salt
Pepper to taste
½ t. thyme
1 t. dried basil
2 cups chicken broth
1 cup water
1 cup evaporated milk
5-6 medium potatoes, peeled
and cubed
½ ring Polish sausage, cubed

Directions:

1. In a dutch oven, melt butter.
2. Saute onions on low heat 3-5 minutes. Add celery, and sauté 5 more minutes.
3. Add bell pepper & corn.
4. Add seasonings, stir well & cover.
5. Reduce heat; simmer for 5 minutes.
6. Add stock, water, potatoes & sausage.
7. Cook until potatoes are soft.
8. Using a blender or food processor, puree about ½ the solids and enough liquid to create smooth consistency.
9. Return to dutch oven & mix remaining solids.
10. About 10 minutes before serving time, add milk.
11. Don't actually cook soup any longer... gently heat to "eating" temperature.

Taco Soup

Contributed By: Rosemarie Parrish

Directions:

1. Cook all over medium heat for at least 30 minutes (I let it cook for at least an hour); occasionally stir.
2. Serve with: Cheddar cheese, Frito's corn chips and Sour cream.

Ingredients:

2½ lbs. ground beef (cooked)
1 large chopped onion
1 can of each of the following (do not drain):
Pinto beans, Kidney beans, Corn, White hominey, Rotel tomatoes (original)
3 cans of stewed tomatoes
1 can of water
1 package of taco seasoning
2 packages of Hidden Valley ranch DIP mix

Potato Sausage Corn Soup

Contributed By: Trish Fox

Ingredients:

2 tbsp butter
½ cup chopped celery
½ cup chopped yellow onion
1 pkg smoked sausage diced
2 cans corn
2 cans diced potatoes
2 cans cream of potato soup
2 cans chicken broth
2 cans whole milk
Crushed black pepper

Directions:

1. Sauté celery and onion in butter until soft.
2. Add sausage and sauté for several minutes.
3. Add all the other ingredients and simmer for 30 minutes til slightly thicker.
4. Add more black pepper to taste and serve.

Vegetable Soup

Contributed By: Sherri Levine

Directions:

1. In a 5 qt non-stick Dutch oven, saute the carrots, onion and celery in olive oil over med/high heat until soft, about 8 minutes.
2. Add all the remaining ingredients except the tomato paste and zucchini and bring to a boil.
3. Cover, reduce the heat to medium/low and simmer for about 30 minutes or until the beans and vegetables are tender.
4. Add the zucchini and cook until tender, about 7 min.

Ingredients:

2 c sliced carrots (4 large)
2 c chopped onion (1 large)
1 c sliced celery (4-5 stalks)
2 T olive oil
¼ c minced garlic (4-5 cloves)
3 cups low sodium vegetable or chicken broth
3 cups tomato juice
1 pound fresh green beans, cut into 1 in pieces
1 pound sugar snap peas
1-15oz can Italian herb seasoned chopped tomatoss
2 T dried basil
2 T dried parsley
1 T dried oregano
1 t Lawry's
¼ t fresh pepper
1 lb. sliced mushrooms, rinsed & drained (optional)
1 small cabbage, chopped
1 large zucchini, sliced and quartered
2-4 tablespoons tomato paste

Spinach Tortellini Soup

Contributed By: Sherri Levine

Ingredients:

1 (10 ounce) package frozen chopped spinach
1 (32 ounce) box chicken broth
2 cups water
1 vegetable bouillon cube
1 (9 ounce) package cheese tortellini
1 tablespoon dried basil
½ tablespoon garlic powder
½ teaspoon Lawry's season salt

Directions:

1. In a large pot over high heat, combine the spinach, chicken broth, water and bouillon cube .
2. Heat to boiling, then reduce heat to low.
3. Stir in remaining ingredients and simmer for 10 to 15 minutes, or until the tortellini is cooked to desired tenderness.

Christine's Red Kidney Bean Soup

Contributed By: Donna Carver

Directions:

1. Sort beans and remove any stones or other material.
2. Rinse beans and throw away the water.
3. With fresh water, add beans to large bowl and soak beans overnight in refrigerator.
4. making sure that water completely covers the top of the beans by a couple of inches.
5. The next day, rinse beans and discard the water.
6. In a saute pan, add olive oil and saute chopped bell peppers, onion and garlic.
7. In a large pot, brown meat on all sides.
8. Add fresh water to pot (6 to 8 cups) to start and continue to add water to pot as beans cook, as needed.
9. Add, canned tomatoes, tomato sauce, orange juice, and chopped tomatoes.
10. Add salt and pepper, to taste.
11. Once the mixture starts to boil put lid on pot but not totally covered.
12. Cook 4 hours.
13. Serve with cooked brown rice.

Ingredients:

1 lb.(16 oz.) dry red kidney beans
1 can Italian tomatoes (14.5 oz.) with basil, garlic and oregano
1 small can tomato sauce (8 oz.)
1 orange (juice)
2 white onions, chopped
2 small red bell peppers, chopped
1 small green bell pepper, chopped
1 green tomato, chopped
3 cloves garlic
salt
pepper
¼ cup extra virgin olive oil
2 pork (or beef) ribs
1 lean pork chop (boneless)
brown rice

Seafood

From fresh water fish to shellfish, there are so many choices.

Orange Roughy Fillets

Contributed by: Kathy Bishop Vaughn

Ingredients:

6 Orange Roughy Fillets
1 T. olive oil
2 cloves garlic
2 T. minced shallots or
green onions
1 t. fresh minced thyme
2 T. lemon juice
3 T. butter
¼ cup wine or vermouth

Directions:

1. Cook filets over high heat in oliver oil.
2. After initial searing, reduce heat & add onions, garlic and wine.
3. Cover to make a sauce. Remove fish and stirring constantly, add lemon juice and thyme.
4. Remove from heat and stir in butter, 1 T. at a time.
5. Pour over fish and serve immediately.

Connie's Shrimp Tacos

Contributed by: Connie Carlson

Directions:

Day Before Meal:

1. Peel and devein shrimp.
2. Put in a gallon zip lock bag or seal container.
3. Add olive oil and Emeril's seasoning to taste.
4. Marinate overnight or at least 4 hours.
5. Combine sour cream, juice from lime, and ½ cup cilantro.
6. Refrigerate overnight.

Day Of Meal:

1. Make Salad: In a jar shake sugar, vinegar, vegetable oil, salt and pepper.
2. Pour over coleslaw and cucumber, mix and refrigerate for at least one hour.
3. Skewer shrimp and grill until pink.
4. For each taco add grilled shrimp, sour cream mixture, fresh cilantro and coleslaw.
5. ENJOY.

Ingredients:

2 lbs shrimp
2 T Olive Oil
1 - 2 T Emeril's Essence Creole Seasoning
1 pt sour cream
1 lime
1 bunch cilantro, cleaned and chopped
1 bag shredded cabbage (coleslaw)
1 cucumber, peeled, cored and diced
⅓ cup sugar
⅓ cup white vinegar
⅓ cup vegetable oil
½ t salt
¼ t pepper
1 package fresh flour tortillas

Salmon in Puff Pastry

Contributed by: Marna Friedman

Ingredients:

4 pieces salmon fillet
  without skin
Puff pastry sheets
1 package Frozen
  Chopped spinach
4 oz. Sour Cream
1 can Cream of
  Mushroom soup
1 medium chopped
  onion
2 cloves chopped garlic
1 t. salt
2T. Olive Oil

Directions:

1. Preheat over to 375.
2. Sauté onions and garlic in 2 T. Olive Oil until clear. Drain liquid.
3. Cook frozen spinach as per package directions. Squeeze excess water.
4. Sauté spinach in onions and garlic mixture. Set aside.
5. Mix sour cream with ½ can Cream of Mushroom soup.
6. Roll out pastry sheet and cut in half.
7. Place ¼ of onion/spinach mixture in center of pastry sheet. Place salmon fillet over mixture and top with sour cream mixture. Wrap pastry sheet around salmon and place in greased pan.
8. Continue for all 4 pieces of salmon fillet.
9. Cook for 30-40 minutes.

Marinated Shrimp

Contributed by: Rachel Konieczny

Directions:

1. Peel shrimp, leaving tails on. Devein if desired.
2. Bring 6 cups of salted water to a boil, add shrimp and cook 3 minutes or just until shrimp turn pink.
3. Drain and rinse with cold water.
4. Chill 2 hours.
5. Combine sugar and next 5 ingredients in a shallow dish.
6. Add shrimp alternately with onion.
7. Cover and chill at least 6 hours, turning often.
8. Drain shrimp and discard marinate before serving.

Ingredients:

2 pounds unpeeled, medium size fresh shrimp
6 cups salted water
½ cup sugar
1½ cups white vinegar
1 cup vegetable oil
¼ cup capers, undrained
1 ½ teaspoon celery salt
½ to 1 teaspoon salt
1 medium size white onion, sliced and separated into rings

Pasta

Who doesn't love pasta? Here are some of our favorite pasta dishes for you to create and enjoy.

Abramo Mac N Cheese

Contributed by: Heather Abramo

Ingredients:

8 oz macaroni noodles
¼ cup flour
¼ cup butter
2 cups milk
Salt to taste
4 oz white American cheese
4 oz cheddar
(I get deli cheese....it melts better)

Directions:

1. Cook the pasta.
2. Melt the butter in a large pan.
3. Add flour gradually keeping it smooth as you go.
4. Gradually add the milk over medium heat until thick and bubbly. Stir in salt and cheese until melted.
5. Stir in with pasta.
6. Bake at 350 for 25 minutes.

World Famous Spaghetti

Contributed by: Tammy Amsler

Directions:

I altered recipe and used 1 lb. sweet Italian sausage and made meatballs as follows:

- 1 lb. ground beef
- ½ cup Italian bread crumbs
- 2 eggs
- 1 tsp. garlic powder
- 1 tsp. salt
- 1 tsp. pepper

Roll mixture into small balls and bake for approximately 20 minutes. Drain grease and add to sauce.

Directions
1. In large, heavy stockpot, brown Italian sausage, breaking up as you stir.
2. Add onions and continue to cook, stirring occasionally until onions are softened.
3. Add garlic, tomatoes, tomato paste, tomato sauce and water.
4. Add basil, parsley, brown sugar, salt, crushed red pepper, and black pepper.
5. Stir well and barely bring to a boil.
6. Stir in red wine.
7. Simmer on low stirring frequently for at least an hour. A longer simmer makes for a better sauce (I use a crock pot on low for at least 5 hours)
8. Cook pasta according to package directions.
9. Spoon sauce over drained spaghetti noodles and sprinkle with parmesan cheese.

Ingredients:

2 lbs Italian sausage, casings removed (mild or hot)
1 small onion, chopped (optional)
3-4 garlic cloves, minced
1 (28 ounce) can diced tomatoes
2 (6 ounce) cans tomato paste
2 (15 ounce) cans tomato sauce
2 cups water (for a long period of simmering time – if simmering for less time add less)
3 tsp. fresh basil
2 tsp. dried parsley flakes
1½ tsp. brown sugar
1 tsp. salt
¼ - ½ tsp. crushed red pepper flakes
¼ tsp. fresh coarse ground black pepper
¼ cup red wine (a good Cabernet!)
1 lb. thin spaghetti or pasta of your choice
Fresh grated parmesan cheese

Lemon Pasta

Contributed by: Heather Abramo

Ingredients:

1 pound pasta (penne or bowtie)
2 T olive oil
1-2 t red pepper flakes
2 cloves minced garlic
Lemon juice from 2 lemons

Directions:

1. Boil a pound of penne pasta (I prefer bowtie).
2. Simmer a couple of tablespoons of olive oil with a teaspoon or two of red pepper flakes and a few cloves of garlic until its fragrant (I like it spicy so I use about three pinches of red pepper flakes and we i love garlic so I use lots...about five cloves chopped...maybe six).
3. Pour the olive oil/flakes/garlic over the pasta and then pour on lemon juice from two freshly squeezed lemons.
4. I usually pan fry chicken with lemon pepper seasoning, chop it up, and toss that into the pasta.

Mac N Cheese

Contributed by: Trish Levy

Directions:

1. Cook noodles according to package directions. Mix all of the above ingredients together and spread into baking dish.

2. Bake at 350 for 40 minutes.

3. Sprinkle with paprika when you get it out of the oven.

Ingredients:

16 oz package cavatappi noodles
4 C shredded cheddar cheese
2 cans Cream of Mushroom soup
2 C mayonnaise
1 medium onion (chopped very fine)

Lasagna

Contributed By: Natalia Armour

Ingredients:

1½ lbs. of ground beef
1 T of vegetable oil
1 large onion
4 cloves of garlic minced
15 oz can of stewed tomatoes
8 oz can of tomato paste
15 oz can of tomato sauce
24 oz cottage cheese
10 oz ricotta cheese
8 oz shredded mozzarella cheese
8 oz shredded parmigiana cheese
Salt, pepper
1 t. dry oregano
1 t. dry basil
½ t. garlic powder
2 T. of fresh chopped flat leaf parsley
2 eggs
1 box of oven-ready lasagna

Directions:

Meat sauce:
Sauté chopped onion and garlic in oil. When translucent, add meat, salt, & pepper. Make sure meat turns brown before you add all cans of tomatoes. Then add dry oregano & basil. Let cook on low heat for about 30 minutes covered. Sauce should thicken.

Cheese mixture:
In a bowl mix cottage cheese, ricotta cheese, parsley, eggs, salt, pepper, 4 oz of parmigiana cheese, ½ teaspoon garlic powder. Mix well.

Assemble lasagna:
Using a 9x13 glass baking dish, place a layer of meat sauce, then layer pasta sheets (don't overlap), then a layer of cheese mixture, then sprinkle some more shredded parmigiana cheese. Repeat layers ending with a layer of meat sauce sprinkled with ½ (4 oz) of the shredded mozzarella.

Bake at 350 for 45 minutes uncovered. Sprinkle leftover mozzarella cheese and bake another 5-10 minutes.
Serve.

Cheesiest Mac N Cheese Ever

Contributed By: Nancy Hayes

Directions:

1. Preheat oven to 300 degrees.
2. Boil pasta per package directions until done and drain.
3. Leave pasta in large saucepan.
4. In another saucepan, melt butter and regular milk, and half of the cheddar (4 cups).
5. Continue to stir, thickening with flour until it is creamy.
6. Pour cheddar mixture over the macaroni in the other pot.
7. Stir in the evaporated milk and eggs.
8. Make layer of the macaroni mixture in the bottom of a large (9X12) casserole dish followed by a layer of both cheeses.
9. Repeat a couple of times. Freezes well at this point if wrapped airtight. Allow to thaw if cooking from frozen.
10. Bake uncovered for an hour or until top is golden brown. You may need to cover with foil to keep from burning.

I usually double this recipe when I make it because it's so good and although the recipe is easy, it's a little time consuming. I get my cheese measured out in separate containers and have a little assembly line set up for when you start doing the layering. Prepare to drool!

Voted best Mac N Cheese by Jessica Gilham!

Ingredients:

16 oz macaroni, whatever shape you want. I usually use bow-tie.
2 lbs sharp cheddar (8 cups - a little more or a little less)
1 lb mozzarella (4 cups - a little more or a little less)
1 stick butter
2 eggs
1 pint regular milk (2 cups)
1 12 oz can evaporated milk
add flour as needed to thicken

Mom's Lasagna Florentine

Contributed By: Abby Hood

Ingredients:

8 oz lasagna noodles (9 full-length noodles)

2 (10 oz) pkgs frozen chopped spinach

4 cups thick spaghetti sauce

4 eggs

2 cups (1 qt) cottage cheese

6 T. minced green onion

2 T. minced parsley

1 tsp. salt (I use less)

1 lb. Mozzarella, grated or thinly sliced

½ cup shredded Parmesan cheese

(Sometimes I add 1lb. of crumbled, cooked, spicy Italian sausage.)

Directions:

1. Cook noodles according to package, drain.
2. Cook spinach according to package, drain thoroughly (I squeeze it dry with my hands).
3. Beat eggs in medium bowl; blend in cottage cheese, spinach, green onion, parsley and salt.
4. Cover bottom of baking dish with 1/4 of sauce. Layer in order 1/3 of the following: noodles, cottage cheese mixture, mozzarella cheese and sauce.
5. Repeat twice with remaining ingredients.
6. Top with Parmesan cheese.
7. Lasagna may now be baked or covered and refrigerated for 1-2 days.
8. Bake at 350 for 30-40 minutes or until bubbly.
9. Let stand 10 minutes before cutting.

One Pan Chicken Alfredo

Contributed By: Alicia Tankersley

Directions:

1. Start by cutting chicken breasts into 1 inch pieces.
2. Season with ½ teaspoon of kosher salt and a few turns of pepper.
3. Brown chicken in olive oil over medium high heat. It does not need to be cooked through at this point.
4. It will continue cooking as it simmers.
5. Once chicken is browned, add minced garlic and sauté for about one minute.
6. Add chicken broth, cream and uncooked pasta to pan and stir.
7. Bring to a boil, then cover and reduce to a simmer for 15-20 minutes until pasta is tender.
8. Remove from heat and stir in shredded parmesan cheese.
9. Season with salt and pepper as needed.

Ingredients:

3 Tablespoons olive oil
1¼ lbs of boneless, skinless chicken breasts
2 cloves of garlic, minced
1 14-oz can of low sodium chicken broth
1 cup heavy cream
½ lb of penne pasta, or any bite-sized shape pasta, uncooked
2 cups freshly shredded real parmesan cheese
Salt and pepper
Flat leaf parsley for garnish

Fabulous Chicken Lasagna

A wonderful dish from my Mom and a favorite for a casserole brigade and family dinner!

Contributed By: Jeff VanHuss

Directions:

1. Preheat oven to 350 degrees.
2. Spray a 13 x 9 glass baking dish with nonstick cooking spray and set aside.
3. In large skillet, heat olive oil over medium heat and add onion and garlic; cook and stir until crisp tender, about 5 minutes.
4. Add mushrooms and bell pepper; cook and stir for about 5 more minutes.
5. Add chicken and remove from heat.
6. In a medium saucepan, combine cream cheese, Alfredo sauce and milk.
7. Cook and stir over low heat until cheese melts and sauce is smooth - stir into chicken mixture.
8. Meanwhile, soak the no boil noodles in cold water for 10 minutes; drain but do not pat dry.
9. In a small bowl, combine the Havarti and Mozzarella cheeses and the cottage cheese.
10. Place ½ cup of the chicken sauce in the bottom of prepared baking dish.
11. Top with one third of the noodles, one third of the chicken mixture, then one third of the mixed cheeses.
12. Repeat layers, ending with cheeses.
13. Sprinkle with Parmesan cheese and Italian Seasoning.
14. Bake for 45 - 55 minutes or until casserole if bubbly and cheeses are melted and starting to brown.
15. This casserole can be prepared, covered and refrigerated for up to 24 hours.
16. If refrigerated, add another 10-15 minutes to baking time. Serves 10!

Ingredients:

1 Tablespoon Olive Oil
1 Chopped Onion
3 Garlic Cloves, minced
1 8 oz. Package of Mushrooms
1 Red Bell Pepper, chopped (optional)
3 Cups Cubed, Cooked Chicken
1 8 oz. Package Cream Cheese, cubed
1 16 oz. Jar Alfredo Sauce
½ Cup of Milk
12 No-Boil Lasagna Noodles
1 Cup Shredded Havarti Cheese
1 Cup Shredded Mozzarella Cheese
½ Cup Grated Parmesan Cheese
1 Cup Cottage Cheese

Cajun Chicken Pasta

Contributed By: Sherri Levine

Directions:

1. Bring a large pot of lightly salted water to a boil.
2. Add linguini pasta, and cook for 8 to 10 minutes, or until al dente; drain.
3. Meanwhile, place chicken and Cajun seasoning in a bowl, and toss to coat.
4. In a large skillet over medium heat, saute chicken in butter until no longer pink and juices run clear, about 5 to 7 minutes.
5. Add bell peppers, mushrooms and onions; cook for 2 to 3 minutes.
6. Reduce heat, and stir in heavy cream.
7. Season the sauce with spices, and heat through.
8. In a large bowl, toss linguini with sauce.
9. Sprinkle with grated Parmesan cheese.
10. Serve with corn bread.

Ingredients:

4 ounces linguine pasta
2 boneless, skinless chicken breast halves, sliced into thin strips
2 teaspoons Cajun seasoning
2 tablespoons butter
1 green bell pepper, chopped
½ red bell pepper, chopped
4 fresh mushrooms, sliced
1 green onion, minced
1½ cups heavy cream
¼ teaspoon dried basil
¼ teaspoon lemon pepper
¼ teaspoon salt
⅛ teaspoon garlic powder
⅛ teaspoon ground black pepper
2 tablespoons grated Parmesan cheese

Poultry

High in protein and big on taste, poultry dishes can be found at breakfast, lunch and dinner!

Quick & Easy Chicken Casserole

Contributed by: Linda Miller

Ingredients:

1 Pkg of Chicken Breast
Tenderloins
1 Can of Cream of
Chicken Soup
1 8 oz Cream Cheese
½ stick of butter
1 sleeve Ritz crackers

Directions:

1. Bake chicken tenderloins with a little salt & butter pat at 350 degrees, 30 min (until tender).
2. Cut up chicken in bite size pieces and line the bottom of casserole dish.
3. Combine and heat cream cheese and Cream of Chicken soup in a sauce pan, stirring constantly.
4. Pour evenly on the cooked chicken tenderloins.
5. Crumble crackers and combine with butter in microwave, stir and pour evenly on top of chicken mixture.

Bake for 30 min at 350 degrees (Cool for 10 minutes before serving).

Savory White Chicken Chili

Contributed by: Kim Jeans

Directions:

1. Drain and rinse the canned white beans. In a medium bowl, mash half of the beans with a potato masher until chunky
2. Reserve the beans until needed.
3. Place chicken stock in pot -- medium heat -- add cannellini beans, white chicken chili mix, corn & diced tomatoes.
4. Defrost bag of grilled chicken & then I cut mine bite size.
5. Once items come to a low boil add chicken -- simmer for 10-12 minutes stirring frequently.
6. Serve the chili in individual bowls topped with a dollop of sour cream, crushed tortilla chips, and shredded cheese.

Ingredients:

2 (14.5-ounce) cans white cannellini beans
Sea salt and freshly ground black pepper
4 cups low-sodium chicken broth
16 oz bag of Tyson Grilled Chicken
¼ cup chopped cilantro leaves
1 can of sweet yellow corn
1 can of diced tomatoes

Toppings on the side:
Sour cream of choice
Tortilla chips or strips, coarsely crushed
1 bag of shredded cheese - flavor of choice - I use mild cheddar

Mouth-Watering Chicken Salad Croissant

Contributed by: Patti Loveless

Ingredients:

2 Boneless, Skinless Chicken Breasts
Mayonnaise
Butter
Salt & Pepper
Grapes, White or Red, chopped in ½'s
Celery, finely chopped
Pecans, Chopped
Freshly baked Croissants

Directions:

1. In frying pan, melt butter and cook chicken breasts until done (use thermometer and do not overcook).
2. Place chicken on cutting board and allow to cool.
3. Cut or shred chicken into small pieces.
4. In a large bowl, mix mayonnaise, grapes, celery and pecans.
5. Fold in chicken, salt and pepper to taste.
6. Add more mayonnaise if needed.
7. Scoop chicken salad onto split croissants.

Dorito Chicken

Contributed by: Renee Tiller

Directions:

1. Combine first 3 ingredients and spread on both sides of chicken.
2. Dredge chicken in crushed chips.
3. Place chicken on lightly greased baking sheet or jellyroll pan.
4. Drizzle with melted butter.
5. Bake at 350 degrees for 20-25 minutes or until chicken is done.

Ingredients:

2 T mayonnaise
¼ tsp salt
¼ tsp dried Italian seasoning
2 skinned and boned chicken breast halves (or 6 boneless chicken tenders works great)
crushed nacho cheese flavored Doritos (about 30)
1 TB butter or margarine, melted

Crockpot Buffalo Chicken Chili

Contributed By: Abby Hood

Ingredients:

2 lb boneless, skinless chicken breasts
1 tablespoon extra virgin olive oil
2 large carrots
3 large celery stalks
5 cloves garlic
5 tablespoons chili powder
2 tablespoons ground cumin
1 tablespoon paprika
½ cup Frank's Red Hot Sauce
2 (15 oz) cans tomato sauce
1 (15 oz) can diced tomatoes
1 (15 oz) can black beans, drained and rinsed
1 (15 oz) can chili beans in sauce (I used Bush's brand which comes in mild, medium or hot. I chose medium. Do NOT drain)
Salt & black pepper to taste

Directions:

1. Heat olive oil in non-stick skillet over medium heat.
2. Add carrots, celery and garlic to food processor (or finely dice).
3. Process vegetables until finely minced.
4. Add the vegetables to the skillet and stir to combine.
5. Cook for 5 minutes until vegetables soften.
6. Add all of the ingredients to crockpot and stir to combine.
7. Cook on high 4-6 hours or low 6-8 hours, until chicken is thoroughly cooked.
8. Remove chicken from crockpot and shred with fork.
9. Return chicken to crockpot and cook additional 15-30 minutes.

Serve immediately with optional toppings: cheese, sour cream, avocado, tortilla chip strips.

Easy Chicken Pot Pie

Contributed by: Tammy Wissing

Directions:

1. Combine first 6 ingredients - spoon into prepared pie crust.
2. Cover with top crust; crimp edges to seal.
3. Slit top crust and brush with egg.
4. Bake at 375 for 40 minutes.
5. Cool for 10 minutes.

Ingredients:

2 cans (10¾ oz) cream of potato soup
1 (16 oz) can of Veg-All mixed vegetables, drained
2 c. cooked, diced chicken (Or canned chunk chicken)
½ tsp. thyme
½ tsp. black pepper
2 (9 inch) frozen pie crusts, thawed (Deep Dish work best)
1 egg, slightly beaten

Chicken Salad

Contributed By: Natalia Armour

Ingredients:

1 rotisserie chicken (buy in store already cooked)
1 cup of mayonnaise
 (you can do more or less whatever you prefer)
3 stalks of celery (chopped finely)
1 large onion
2 chopped scallions
1 tablespoon of chopped dill
½ juiced lemon
¼ cup of toasted chopped walnuts
½ cup of red grapes chopped
½ tablespoon of chopped parsley
salt, pepper

Directions:

1. Cut chicken into small pieces.
2. Mix mayonnaise with salt, pepper, and lemon juice.
3. Add all ingredients together and mix with mayonnaise mixture.
4. Chill and enjoy!

Stuffed Chicken Breasts

Contributed By: Kathy Bishop Vaughan

Directions:

1. Mix goat cheese, herbs, parsley, salt & pepper, and set aside for later.
2. Make a slit down the side of 6 chicken breasts, creating pockets.
3. Spoon a layer of cheese mix inside and close (use toothpicks to hold slit together if needed).
4. Sauté in 1/4 c. oil over medium heat for approximately 8 minutes on each side. Check for doneness. Remove chicken.
5. Add 4 cloves chopped garlic, 1/2 c. chopped sundried tomatoes and 1 c heavy cream to pan
6. Scrape all bits off the bottom of pan.
7. Bring to a boil; simmer 5 minutes.
8. Spoon sauce over chicken.

Ingredients:

6 chicken breasts
1 cup goat cheese
1 t. dried Italian herbs (Good Seasons)
1 t. chopped fresh Parsley
Salt & pepper to taste
4 cloves chopped garlic
1/2 c. chopped sundried tomatoes
1 c heavy cream

Mexican Lasagna

Contributed By: Mary Pierce

Ingredients:

3 Tablespoons olive Oil
2 pounds ground chicken
2 Tablespoons chili Powder
2 teaspoons ground cumin
1 bottle(regular size) taco sauce
(I replaced with salsa)
1 15 ounce can of Black Beans
(drained)
1 small bag of frozen corn
salt and pepper to taste.
(I used Mrs. Dash)
2 1/2 cups of shredded cheese
sliced black olives (optional)
8 inch soft flour tortillas

Directions:

1. Preheat oven 425 degrees F.
2. In a pan, use 1 tablespoon of olive oil, and cook the 2 pounds of ground chicken with cumin, chili powder and a little salt and pepper. Cook until done
3. Add taco sauce (or salsa), black beans and corn. taste. Make sure you don't need any more salt and pepper or Mrs. Dash
4. Coat a shallow backing dish with other tablespoon of oil. (I used a regular size casserole dish)
5. Cut the tortillas in quarters for easy layering.
6. Start with a layer of the meat mixture, layer of cheese, layer of tortillas, repeat 2 times more...... do not use too many tortillas because they will suck up the juice too much.
7. Bake lasagna 12-15 minutes or until cheese is slightly brown.

Chicken & Mushroom Sauce

Contributed By: Mary Pierce

Directions:

1. Place each chicken breast half between 2 sheets of heavy-duty plastic wrap, and pound to ½-inch thickness using a meat mallet or small heavy skillet.
2. Heat a large nonstick skillet over medium-high heat.
3. Add canola oil to pan; swirl to coat.
4. Sprinkle chicken with ¼ teaspoon salt and pepper.
5. Add chicken to pan; cook 3 minutes on each side or until done.
6. Transfer chicken to a serving platter; keep warm.
7. Add shallots and mushrooms to pan; sauté for 4 minutes or until browned, stirring occasionally.
8. Add garlic; sauté for 1 minute, stirring constantly.
9. Stir in wine, scraping pan to loosen browned bits; bring to a boil.
10. Cook until liquid almost evaporates.
11. Sprinkle mushroom mixture with remaining ¼ teaspoon salt and flour; cook 30 seconds, stirring frequently.
12. Add broth to pan; bring to a boil.
13. Cook 2 minutes or until slightly thick.
14. Remove pan from heat; add butter and thyme, stirring until butter melts.
15. Serve with chicken.

Ingredients:

4 (6-ounce) skinless, boneless chicken breast halves
2 teaspoons canola oil
½ teaspoon salt, divided
¼ teaspoon freshly ground black pepper
¼ cup chopped shallots
1 (8-ounce) package pre-sliced mushrooms
2 minced garlic cloves
½ cup dry white wine
1½ teaspoons all-purpose flour
¾ cup fat-free, lower-sodium chicken broth
2 tablespoons butter
1 t minced fresh thyme

Rick's Crumbly Chicken

Contributed By: Laura Miller Edwards

Ingredients:

8 chicken tenderloins
1 stick of butter, melted
1 sleeve of Keebler townhouse crackers

Directions:

1. In a 9x9 pan, lay out chicken tenders flat. In a baggie, crush crackers leaving some small chunks.
2. Sprinkle evenly over the top of the chicken.
3. Evenly pour melted butter over the top of the chicken.
4. Bake at 350 degrees for 30 minutes.

Easy and Quick. Kids (big and small) LOVE this!

Chicken & Rice Casserole

Contributed By: Tammy Wissing

Directions:

1. Cook Minute rice in microwave.
2. Cook frozen broccoli in microwave.
3. Mix cooked rice, cooked broccoli, chicken, Cream of Celery soup, Cream of Chicken soup, salt and pepper into casserole dish.
4. Sprinkle with shredded cheese.
5. Bake uncovered for about 30 minutes on 350.

Ingredients:

1 can Cream of Celery soup
1 can Cream of Chicken soup
2 cups diced, cooked chicken
(or canned chunk chicken)
4 servings Minute Rice
½ - 1 bag frozen broccoli
salt and pepper
2 cups shredded cheese

Denise's Poppy Seed Chicken

Contributed By: Denise Hutchinson

Ingredients:

4 large boneless chicken breasts
1 can Cream of Chicken soup (undiluted)
2 cups sour cream

1 stack Ritz crackers crushed (or saltines)
½ stick margarine melted
2 tsp poppy seed
salt and pepper to taste

Directions:

1. Cook chicken until tender, cool and cut into bite sized pieces.
2. Mix with Cream of Chicken soup and sour cream.
3. Mix well and place in a 9x13 inch casserole sprayed with a nonstick spray.

For Topping:
4. Mix the crushed crackers, melted margarine and poppy seeds.
5. Spread on top of casserole and bake at 350 for 30 to 40 minutes until lightly browned and bubbly in center.

Optional:
6. You can spread a layer of any vegetable you like in the bottom of the casserole before you put in the chicken mixture.
7. Peas are good. Also corn and lima beans work well.

Swiss Chicken

Contributed By: Mandi Bagwell

Directions:

1. Spray crock pot with cooking spray.
2. Place chicken on bottom of pot.
3. Top with cheese.
4. Combine soup and milk and spoon over cheese.
5. Sprinkle with stuffing mix.
6. Drizzle melted butter over top.
7. Cook on low for 8-10 hours or high for 4-6 hours.

Ingredients:

6 boneless, chicken breasts
6 slices of swiss cheese
1 can Cream of Mushroom soup
¼ cup of milk
2 cup herb stuffing mix
½ cup melted butter

Chicken Broccoli Braid

Contributed By: Patti Loveless

Ingredients:

1 Roll Original Pillsbury Croissants
½ Cup Sour Cream
2 Cups Chicken, cooked, shredded
¾ Cup Cheddar Cheese, Grated
1 Can Cream of Mushroom Soup
1 tsp Dried Thyme
1 Cup Broccoli, cooked
Salt & Pepper

Directions:

1. Preheat oven to 375°.
2. Roll croissants out flat on a greased or nonstick cookie sheet.
3. Squeeze perforations together so rolls do not split.
4. Using a pizza cutter, make 2" cuts every inch or so down the left side of the croissants.
5. Do the same down the right side of the croissants, even with the cuts on the left side, making sure not to connect with the cuts on the left.
6. There should be an uncut strip of croissant down the center.
7. Mix together the chicken, soup, sour cream, cheese, thyme and broccoli.
8. Place mixture down the center of the croissant, leaving an inch on each end.
9. Carefully lift croissant strip from each side, bring over center of mixture, twist around each other once, place strip down to the side and press firmly.
10. Repeat until all strips are crossed over mixture.
11. Bake for 10 minutes or until croissant is golden brown.
12. Cook for 5 minutes and slice to serve.

Avocado Artichoke Pesto-Stuffed Chicken

Contributed By: Beth Haigh

Directions:

1. In high-speed food processor or blender (think VitaMix,) add avocado, fresh basil, cottage cheese, lemon juice, crushed garlic and seasonings.
2. Blend until smooth.
3. Stir in chopped artichokes.
4. Place in fridge until needed.
5. Preheat oven to 350°F.
6. Butterfly chicken breasts. (Cut breast in half horizontally but not all the way through so still in one piece.)
7. In baggie or small bowl, combine the basil, thyme, onion, red pepper flakes, garlic powder and salt.
8. Sprinkle rub mixture on both sides of each breast and place on parchment-lined jelly roll pan.
9. Place ¼ pesto mixture in each breast and fold top half of breast to "close."
10. Cook for about 20 minutes, or until chicken is done.
11. Let rest for 5 minutes before serving.

Ingredients:

2 Haas avocados
½ cup chopped organic fresh basil
¼ cup 4% milk-fat cottage cheese
1 Tbsp organic lemon juice
1 tsp crushed organic garlic
1 tsp fine grind organic black pepper
½ tsp fine grind Himalayan salt
½ tsp organic cayenne pepper
½ tsp organic paprika
7 oz artichoke hearts, chopped
4 large organic chicken breasts, butterflied
1 Tbsp organic dried basil
1 Tbsp organic dried thyme
1 Tbsp organic dried onion, powder or minced
1 tsp crushed red pepper flakes
1 tsp organic garlic powder
1 tsp Himalayan salt

Turkey & Vegetable Chili

Contributed By: Melissa Gilbert

Ingredients:

2 T olive oil
1 large sweet onion, diced
2 carrots diced
1 red pepper diced
1 zucchini or squash diced
4 cloves garlic, crushed
1½ pounds ground turkey
1 (28-ounce) can crushed tomatoes
1 cup beer (dark preferred)
3 tablespoons chili powder
1 teaspoon curry powder
3 tablespoons hot sauce
⅓ cup honey
1 (10-ounce) package frozen corn
1 (15-ounce) can pink or kidney beans
1 (15-ounce) can black beans, drained
¼ cup diced mild green chiles
3 beef bouillon cubes

2 tablespoons flour (optional)

Directions:

1. Heat oil in large skillet over medium-low heat.
2. Add vegetables and cook for 5 minutes, stirring frequently.
3. Add garlic and cook 2 minutes.
4. Add turkey and cook until no pink remains. Drain.
5. Add tomatoes, beer, chili powder, curry powder, hot sauce, honey, corn, beans, chiles, bouillon cubes and flour, stirring until mixed.
6. Transfer mixture to slow cooker or crockpot
7. Cover and cook on low for 8 to 10 hours or on high for 4 to 6 hours.

Chicken Rice-a-Roni Casserole

Contributed By: Trish Fox

Directions:

1. Cook rice as per package.
2. Turn off heat and mix in soup.
3. Layer chicken and rice in a buttered pan.
4. Top with buttered ritz crackers.
5. Bake at 350 for 20-25 minutes.

Ingredients:

2-3 cups shredded chicken
1 family size box
chicken rice-a-roni
1 family size can
Cream of Chicken soup
2 tbsp butter, melted
1 sleeve Ritz crackers, crushed

White Chicken Chili

Contributed By: Cheryl Wheatley

Ingredients:

4 skinless chicken breasts
4 cups chicken stock
1 clove garlic, minced
1 medium onion, diced
1 (15 ounce) can white beans
with liquids from beans
1 (4 ounce) can diced green
chilis with liquids from chilis
1 teaspoon dried oregano
1 teasponn ground cumin
½ teaspoon chili powder
1 teaspoon ground black
pepper
1 teaspoon salt
1 teaspoon chopped fresh
oregano

Directions:

1. Add chicken to a 4-quart heavy bottomed dutch oven or stock pot.
2. Add chicken stock and cook until tender, about 15 minutes.
3. Shred chicken with two forks and then add back to the liquid.
4. Add garlic and onion to stockpot, white beans, green chilis, dried oregano, cumin, chili powder, salt, pepper and chopped fresh oregano. Stir until well combined.
5. Taste for flavor and adjust to your preference
6. Simmer over low heat for about 5 hours.
7. Remove from heat and serve.

Crockpot Mexican Chicken

Contributed By: Millie Ann Morrell

Directions:

1. Put it all in a crockpot in that order.
2. Cook on low for 6-8 hrs.
3. Remove chicken, shred it all, and return to crockpot.
4. Add some hot sauce to taste.
5. Stir it up and serve how you would like.

Ingredients:

Can of black beans, drained
Can of mexicorn, drained
Three boneless, skinless
chicken breasts
Packet of taco seasoning
16 oz jar of salsa

Lemon Chicken

Contributed By: Katrice Edwards

Ingredients:

4 chicken breasts with skin on
2 lemons
fresh thyme
½ cup very good tasting olive oil
½ cup very good tasting dry white wine
teaspoon of kosher salt
2 T fresh garlic crushed

Directions:

1. Preheat oven to 350
2. Season chicken with salt and pepper.
3. In small sauce pan, put in olive oil and garlic; let simmer until you smell garlic then add wine, thyme, lemon zest, and squeeze two tablespoons of lemon and garlic.
4. Get a flat glass bowl for the oven and add the sauce in the bottom , then place breasts on top.
5. Apply more olive oil to the chicken breast skin so it will crisp up in the oven.
6. Cut up the second lemon and tuck it under the chicken breast and add more crushed garlic around the chicken.
7. Bake for 30-40 minutes.
8. Take out of oven and cover with aluminium foil and let it rest for 10 minutes

Cheater's Quick Greek

Contributed By: Deanna Morrell

Directions:

1. Prepare garlic shells.
2. Add a tablespoon of water at the end of cooking if needed to keep sauce a little thinner.
3. Add all ingredients and stir well.
4. Feel free to add additional ingredients if desired.
5. Serve with fresh fruit and garlic bread.

Ingredients:

Can of black beans, drained
Can of mexicorn, drained
Three boneless, skinless chicken
1 pkg of Knorr garlic shells, prepare as directed
1 lg chicken breast, cooked & cubed
1 small can of mushrooms (sliced) drained
1 small bottle of artichoke hearts, drained
5 sun-dried tomatoes, chopped
1 small can of sliced black olives, drained
1 cup of chopped broccoli and/or green beans
Packet of taco seasoning
16 oz jar of salsa

White Chicken Chili

Contributed By: Jeff VanHuss

Ingredients:

32 oz. box of Chicken Stock
3 Cans of Cannelini or White
Northern beans, undrained
5 Cups of Cooked Chicken,
shredded or chopped
1 16 oz. jar of Salsa - adjust the
heat of the salsa to personal
taste
1 Small box of Velveeta cheese,
cubed (Queso Velveeta cheese
may be used)
1 8 oz. bag of shredded Pepper
Jack cheese (2% cheese works
well!)

1 McCormick White Chicken
Chili packet provides perfect
spices for chili!

Directions:

1. Add all ingredients to a crockpot or large soup pot until cheese is melted.
2. Allowing the chili to simmer for several hours enhances the flavor and is even better the next day!
3. Garnish with sour cream and green onions, if desired, and may be served with crackers, cornbread or tortilla chips.

White Chicken Chili

Contributed By: Rachel Konieczny

Directions:

1. Cube chicken.
2. Cover with water and boil until tender, drain. (If you prefer you can sauté the chicken in a bit of olive oil)
3. In a huge pot, sauté onions in oil. Stir in garlic, chilies, cumin, oregano, cloves, cilantro and stir tor two minutes.
4. Add beans, chicken and chicken broth.
5. Bring to a boil.
6. Finish with cheese, by stirring in only a few minutes before serving.
7. Top with garnishes!

Ingredients:

3 cans or 1 lb. dried and prepared Great Northern Beans
1-2 lbs. chicken breasts
2 cans chicken broth
1 Tbsp. olive oil
2 medium onions (chopped)
4 garlic cloves (minced)
2 4-oz. cans chopped green chilies
2 tsp. fresh or dried oregano
¼ tsp. ground cloves
¼ tsp. cumin
¼ tsp. cayenne pepper
1 lb. Monterey jack cheese
For garnish: sour cream, salsa, fresh cilantro, jalapenos

Chicken & Dumplings

Contributed By: Mandi Bagwell

Ingredients:

Whole chicken
3-4 eggs
Stick of butter
1 cup of milk
Salt & Pepper (to taste)
10 cups of flour (half plain half self-rising)
Buttermilk
10 T shortening

Directions:

1. In a large pot boil whole chicken & eggs, salt & pepper with enough water to cover.
2. Boil for 1 hour.
3. When chicken is done, take it out of water and set aside to cook for a bit.
4. Peel & cut eggs and add them back to broth.
5. When cool enough, pick chicken from bone & add back to broth.
6. Add 1 stick of butter & milk to broth and cook on medium while you are mixing dumplings.
7. In a large bowl cut in 10 tablespoons of shortening to 10 cups of flour.
8. Stir in buttermilk until biscuit dough consistency.
9. Roll out and cut in to strips.
10. Cut in bite size pieces and set aside.
11. Increase heat to boiling.
12. Add dumplings, stirring frequently (do not let them stick together).
13. Also, if water is not boiling when you drop them, they will stick together.
14. After all dumplings are added, reduce heat to low and cook covered for about 30 minutes.
15. Should serve 10 or more people......

Crockpot Creamy Chicken

Contributed By: Sherri Levine

Directions:

1. Spray crockpot with nonstick spray.
2. Soften cream cheese in microwave.
3. Place in crockpot and mix with italian dressing mix, water, and soup.
4. Use immersion blender to make smooth.
5. Add chicken and stir to cover.
6. Cover, cook on low 6-8hrs, or high 4-6 hrs.
7. Serve with a crusty loaf of french bread.

Ingredients:

1½ lb chicken breast, cut as desired
1½ blocks cream cheese
1-23 oz can Cream of Chicken soup
2 cups chicken broth
2 packages Good Seasons Italian Dressing mix

Miss Jess' Chicken Casserole

Contributed By: Jessica Gilham

Ingredients:

1 lb. chicken breasts
1 medium onion diced
1 sleeve Ritz crackers, crumbled
2 cups grated cheddar cheese
Butter
8 oz sour cream
1 16 oz can Cream of Chicken and Mushroom soup
1 tsp paprika
1 clove garlic minced
½ cup chicken broth
Salt and pepper to taste

Directions:

1. Preheat oven to 350.
2. Boil chicken breasts until no longer pink - about 12 minutes.
3. On medium heat, cook onion and garlic in a pan until soft.
4. In a baking dish, cover the bottom of the dish with ¾ of the Ritz cracker sleeve.
5. Put several small pats of butter on the the crackers. Not more than 3 tbsp.
6. Shred chicken and layer on top of the butter and crackers.
7. Mix together onions, garlic, sour cream, cream of chicken soup, paprika, salt, pepper, and chicken broth.
8. Pour mixture over chicken.
9. Spread shredded cheese on top.
10. Sprinkle remaining Ritz crumbs on top.
11. Bake uncovered 25 minutes.

Buttermilk Baked Chicken

This is the tastiest chicken for a cold winter's night! Family favorite!!

Contributed By: Jeff VanHuss

Directions:

1. Melt butter in a lightly greased 13 x 9 inch baking dish in a 425 degree oven.
2. Remove dish from oven and set aside.
3. Dip chicken in ½ cup of the buttermilk and then dredge in flour.
4. Arrange the chicken in the heated dish and bake at 425 degrees for 25 minutes.
5. Turn the chicken and bake for 10 more minutes.
6. While cooking, stir together remaining 1 cup buttermilk and the soups; season with spices and a splash of white wine or chicken broth.
7. Pour mixture over the chicken and cook for another 10 - 15 minutes.
8. This dish can be garnished with lemon wedges or caramelized French's onions! Enjoy

Ingredients:

¼ C butter or margarine
4 Boneless, skinless chicken breasts
1½ C buttermilk, divided (Reduced Fat Buttermilk will work fine!)
¾ C All-Purpose Flour (Wheat flour may also be used)
1 Can Healthy Request Cream of Chicken Soup
1 Can Healthy Request Cream of Mushroom Soup
1 8 oz. Carton of Fresh Mushrooms
Salt and Pepper and other Herbs for Taste
White wine or chicken broth

Grilled Chicken Marinade

Contributed By: Alicia Tankersley

Ingredients:

4 boneless, skinless chicken breasts (about 1¾ pounds total)
6 tablespoons extra virgin olive oil
4 large garlic cloves, minced
1 teaspoon dried thyme
½ teaspoon dried oregano
1¼ teaspoon salt
½ teaspoon freshly ground black pepper
1½ teaspoons lemon zest, from one lemon

Directions:

1. Trim chicken and set aside.
2. Mix remaining ingredients in a gallon ziploc bag.
3. Add chicken and marinate overnight or at least 2 hours in the refrigerator.
4. Remove from marinade and grill.

Chicken & Dumplings

Contributed By: Sherri Levine

Directions:

1. Combine all stew ingredients in a large pot; bring to a boil.
2. Reduce heat, cover pot, and simmer until chicken is no longer pink in the center and the vegetables are tender, 30 to 40 minutes.
3. Remove bay leaf.
4. In medium bowl, stir Bisquick mix and the milk with fork until soft dough forms.
5. Drop dough by spoonfuls onto hot chicken mixture (do not drop directly into liquid).
6. Cook uncovered over low heat 10 minutes.
7. Cover and cook 10 minutes longer.

Ingredients:

Stew:
4 c chicken broth
1 lb chicken breast, cubed
1 onion, chopped
8 ounces baby carrots
2 stalks celery, chopped
1 bay leaf
2 T fresh or 2 t parsley flakes
Salt, pepper, onion powder to taste

Dumplings:
1 c Bisquick
⅓ c milk

Chicken Club Brunch Braid

Contributed By: Sherri Levine

Ingredients:

½ cup mayonnaise
1 tablespoon minced fresh parsley
2 teaspoons Dijon mustard
1½ teaspoons finely chopped onion (no onion for kids)
1 lb chicken
4 bacon strips
1 cup (4 ounces) shredded Swiss cheese, divided
2 tubes refrigerated crescent rolls
2 plum tomatoes
2 cups shredded lettuce

Directions:

1. If using pre cooked chicken, cut into bite size pieces. If fresh, cook chicken and cut into 1/2-inch cubes
2. In a large bowl, combine the mayonnaise, parsley, mustard and onion.
3. Stir in the chicken, bacon and ¾ cup cheese.
4. Heat oven to 375°F.
5. Spray cookie sheet with cooking spray.
6. Unroll both cans of dough into 2 large rectangles.
7. Place dough with long sides together on cookie sheet, forming 15x12-inch rectangle.
8. Press edges and perforations to seal.
9. Spoon and spread chicken mixture lengthwise in 6-inch-wide strip down center of dough.
10. Slice half of a tomato; place over filling.
11. With scissors or sharp knife, make cuts 1½ inches apart on long sides of dough to within ½ inch of filling.
12. Twisting each strip once, alternately cross strips over filling.
13. Tuck short ends under; press to seal.
14. Bake 28 to 33 minutes or until golden brown.
15. Sprinkle with remaining cheese. Let stand for 5 minutes.
16. Cut crosswise into slices.
17. Place lettuce around braid; sprinkle with chopped tomato and serve warm with dijon mustard-flavored mayonnaise.

Beef and more

Beef isn't alone here. Our Realtors® create recipes with Lamb, Pork, Veal and Venison too!

Magically Easy Beef Stew

Contributed by: Tammy Amsler

Ingredients:

2 lbs. stew meat
2 onions, chopped
2 celery stalks, chopped
2 garlic cloves, minced
2-3 carrots, sliced
2-3 potatoes, peeled and cubed
2 tsp. salt
1 tsp. sugar
1 bay leaf
½ tsp. black pepper
3 Tbsp. minute tapioca
2 Tbsp. fresh parsley
2 cups tomato juice or V-8 juice

Directions:

1. Put meat in a large oven proof dish, put vegetables on top of meat.
2. Combine last 8 ingredients with juice and pour over meat and vegetables.
3. Do not stir!
4. Cover tightly and bake at 275° for 4 hours.

Haigh Hash

Contributed by: Beth Haigh

Directions:

1. In a large skillet, brown beef with onion until cooked to medium. Drain.
2. Add sweet potatoes, garlic, cumin, parsley, salt, pepper and cook till sweet potatoes are tender, about 10 minutes longer.
3. Add in spinach and cook only until spinach lightly wilted, a few minutes longer.

Note: The beef and onion can be cooked and the potatoes peeled/cubed ahead of time.

Ingredients:

1 lb grass-fed ground beef
½ of a large red onion, chopped
1 cup peeled and cubed sweet potatoes
1 tsp minced fresh organic garlic
½ – 1 tsp organic ground cumin (to taste)
1 tsp organic dried parsley
½ tsp Himalayan salt
¼ tsp organic ground black pepper
2-3 cups organic baby spinach

Porcupine Meatballs

Contributed by: Rebecca Singer

Ingredients:

¼ cup tomato soup
(not reconstituted)
1 pound ground beef
¼ cup uncooked rice
1 egg
¼ cup finely chopped onion
2 tablespoons parsley
1 teaspoon salt

Directions:

Mix all ingredients together.
Form into balls about 1½ inches across.
Brown on all sides.
Cover with the remaining tomato soup with at least 1 cup water.
Simmer for 40 minutes.

Beef Steak in Mushroom Gravy

Contributed by: Heather Abramo

Directions:

1. In small bowl, combine flour, onion, and parsley. Coat steaks on both sides in flour mixture.
2. In large skillet sprayed with cooking spray, lightly brown steaks for 3 minutes on each side.
3. In large bowl, combine mushroom soup, mushrooms, beef broth, and any remaining flour mixture. Pour soup mixture evenly over steaks.
4. Bring mixture to a boil. Lower heat. Cover and simmer for 20-25 minutes or until steaks are tender.
5. When serving, evenly spoon gravy over steaks.

Ingredients:

6 T. all purpose flour
1 t. dried onion flakes
1 t. dried parsley
4 4 oz lean minute
or cube steaks
1 can of Healthy Request
Cream of Mushroom Soup
½ cup sliced mushrooms
1 14.4 oz can Swanson
Beef Broth

Spaghetti & Meat Sauce

Contributed By: Natalia Armour

Ingredients:

1½ pounds of ground meat
1 large onion chopped
3 cloves of garlic finely chopped
1 28 ounce can of tomato sauce
1 6 ounce can of tomato paste
1 12.5 ounce can of crushed
tomatoes
1 tablespoon of fresh basil
Salt, pepper,
½ teaspoon of dry oregano and
basil each

Directions:

1. Sauté onions and garlic until translucent.
2. Add meat, salt & pepper, and let the meat turn brown.
3. Stir constantly to make sure all meat is brown.
4. Then add all tomato cans, spices, and let simmer covered for 25-30 minutes.
5. Add basil.
6. Cook your favorite pasta and serve the sauce on top.

Taco Twist

Contributed by: Joshua Chapman

Directions:

1. Brown meat and onions.
2. Drain.
3. Add taco seasoning mix and tomato sauce.
4. Boil and then turn heat off.
5. Cook and drain the box of rotini pasta.
6. Once drained, add 1 cup sour cream and 1 cup shredded cheese and mix well.
7. Place noodle mixture in a 2 quart casserole dish.
8. Top with meat mixture and remaining ½ cup of cheese.
9. Bake at 350 for 30 minutes.

Ingredients:

1 chopped onion
1 pound ground beef (or ground turkey)
1 package taco seasoning mix
1 15 oz. can tomato sauce
1 cup sour cream
1½ cups shredded cheddar cheese
1 box of rotini pasta

Fall Off The Bone Mesquite-Spiced Oven Baked Ribs

Contributed By: Priscilla Johnson

Ingredients:

3 lb pork baby back ribs
Salt & Pepper
Grill Masters Smokehouse
Maple Seasoning
Lawry's Mesquite Marinade
BBQ Sauce
Aluminum Foil

Directions:

1. Preheat oven to 350.
2. Spread aluminum foil on cooking sheet.
3. Lightly drizzle olive oil or non-stick spray on foil.
4. After rinsing ribs, season both sides with Salt, Pepper, & Smokehouse Maple seasoning.
5. Cover the top with aluminum foil and cook covered for 1½ hrs.
6. Uncover ribs and add Lawry's Mesquite Marinade on top of ribs.
7. Cook an additional 30 minutes, uncovered.

Ribs will be ready to serve. To add extra tenderness, turn OFF the oven and re-cover the ribs and allow them to stay in the oven an additional 15-20 minutes.

Sloppy Joes

Contributed by: Valerie Davis

Directions:

1. Brown beef in a large skillet.
2. While beef is browning, in a separate bowl, mix together ketchup, red pepper puree and brown sugar.
3. Drain beef.
4. Using the same skillet, heat up the olive oil to medium high heat and cook the onions until translucent, about 5 minutes.
5. Add in the garlic and chili powder and cook for another 2-3 minutes.
6. Add the beef mixture back into the pan.
7. Stir in ketchup mixture and heat through, approximately 5 minutes.

Ingredients:

2 pounds lean ground beef
2 tablespoons olive oil
1 small to medium yellow onion, minced
4 garlic cloves, minced
2-3 teaspoons chili powder
½ jar of roasted red peppers, pureed
1 cup ketchup
2 teaspoons dark brown sugar

Beef Stroganoff

Contributed By: Tammy Wissing

Ingredients:

1½ lb round steak, cut in cubes
½ stick margarine
1 can water
1 medium onion, chopped
2 Tbsp. plain flour
1 can cream of chicken soup
1 small can mushrooms or 8 oz fresh sliced mushrooms
salt and pepper to taste
½ pt. sour cream

Directions:

1. Brown beef in butter.
2. Add onion and brown slightly.
3. Add flour and stir until smooth.
4. Add soup, water and sliced mushrooms.
5. Cover and simmer for 45 minutes.
6. Remove from heat.
7. Add sour cream.
8. Serve over egg noodles.

Island Flank Steak

Contributed by: Trish Fox

Directions:

1. Mix marinade and pour over meat.
2. Let stand on the counter for 2 hours.
3. Thread meat on skewers and grill.

Ingredients:

2-3 lb flank steak cut in strips
½ cup soy sauce
¼ cup brown sugar
2 tbsp olive oil
1 tbsp chopped garlic
2 tsp dried ginger (or more if you prefer)
Cracked black pepper
6 oz pineapple juice

Sweet-Hot Jalapeno Ribs

Contributed By: Alicia Tankersley

Ingredients:

2 (16-oz) cans pinto beans, drained
3 lbs country-style pork ribs
½ teaspoon garlic powder
½ teaspoon salt
½ teaspoon pepper
1 medium onion, chopped
1 (10.5 oz) jar red jalapeno jelly
1 (5 oz) bottle steak sauce
2 jalapeno peppers, seeded and finely chopped (optional)

Directions:

1. Place pinto beans in a 4-qt electric slow cooker and set aside.
2. Cut ribs apart, if necessary. Sprinkle with garlic powder, salt and pepper.
3. Place ribs on a rack in broiler pan.
4. Broil 5 ½ inches from heat (with electric oven door partially opened) 18-20 minutes or until well browned, turning once.
5. Add ribs to slow cooker, and sprinkle with onion.
6. Combine jelly, steak sauce, and, if desired, chopped pepper in a saucepan; cook over low heat until jelly melts.
7. Pour over ribs; stir gently.
8. Cover and cook on high 5-6 hours or cook on high 1 hour and then reduce to low 8-9 hours.
9. Remove ribs; skim fat from sauce.
10. Cook sauce with beans, uncovered, on high 30 minutes or until slightly thickened.
11. Add ribs just before searving to reheat.

Monique's Perfect Bite Chili

Contributed By: Monique Csoke

Directions:

1. Saute ground beef with onion until brown, drain fat.
2. Cook chili first on stove and add everything into large pot and cook on Medium High, stirring frequently.
3. Add to Crock Pot on Low for 8-10 hours.
4. Turn off heat and let sit overnight.
5. Turn on low next morning and serve that night or next day, gets better with age.

Serve over Crumbled Corn bread in bottom of bowl, chili, then shredded cheddar, sour cream, avocado, tortilla strips* (I make my own) sour cream and fresh lime juice last 2 bay leaf (remove before serving)

You may thicken, add flour and water paste in chili after all mixed
*Buy corn tortillas, cut thin strips and fry quickly in canola oil.

Ingredients:

2 lbs. Ground Meat
1 onion diced
2 Alarm Chili Mix (Wick Fowlers, all spices in here)
3-4 Cans Dark Red Kidney Beans
Diced Tomatoes (optional)
1 Family Size Campbell's Tomato Soup
1 tsp garlic minced or paste (Publix sells in vegetable aisle on wall)
Fixin's:
2 limes
Sour Cream
Tortilla Strips
Avocado diced
Shredded Cheddar
Jiffy Corn Bread (cook in iron skillet)

Hamburger Rice Casserole

Contributed By: Denise Hutchinsin

Ingredients:

2 (16-oz) cans pinto beans, drained
3 lbs country-style pork ribs
½ teaspoon garlic powder
½ teaspoon salt
½ teaspoon pepper
1 medium onion, chopped
1 (10.5 oz) jar red jalapeno jelly
1 (5 oz) bottle steak sauce
2 jalapeno peppers, seeded and finely chopped (optional)
1½ pound chopped hamburger seasoned with salt & pepper
1 small onion, chopped
1 cup Minute Rice
1 cup water
1 cup chopped celery
1 cup Cream of Chicken soup
1 cup Cream of Mushroom soup
1 teaspoon soy sauce

Directions:

1. Brown hamburger & onion. Drain well.
2. Add salt, pepper, rice and celery and continue to brown a few minutes longer
3. Mix soups, water and soy sauce in casserole dish.
4. Add meat mixture.
5. Bake 30 minutes at 350.

Chili Meat Loaf

Contributed By: Jeff Buffo

Directions:

1. Combine the first 7 ingredients and simmer for 5 minutes.
2. Combine half of the sauce with the other ingredients and form the loaf.
3. Bake 30 minutes at 350 degrees
4. Pour remaining sauce over the meatloaf and bake an additional 20-30 minutes.

Ingredients:

1 Cup Tomato Sauce
2 Tablespoons Brown Sugar
1 Tsp Worcestershire Sauce
1 Tsp Vinegar
½ Tsp Dried Mustard
½ - 1 Tsp Chili Powder
½ Tsp salt
1-2 lbs. Ground Beef
½ Cup evaporated milk
½ Cup Bread Crumbs
¼ Onion

Carole's Cream Chipped Beef on Toast

Contributed By: Dianne Piecuch

Ingredients:

4 Tablespoons butter
4 Tablespoons all-purpose flour
2 cups milk (to desired thickness)
2 packages Carl Buddig beef - cut in small ½" pieces
Pepper (to taste)
Bread

Directions:

1. Melt butter in saucepan, then slowly stir in flour and milk, trying to keep lumps to a minimum.
2. Keep stirring consistently until mixture is smooth and thickens. (You can add a little milk as needed, so start with a little less.)
3. Once the mixture has thickened, stir in Carl Buddig beef pieces.
4. There is already salt in the beef, so you may not need salt at all, but add pepper to taste.
5. Toast bread slices in toaster.
6. Serve hot cream chipped beef over toast slices.

Sausage Pinwheels

Contributed By: Teena Regan

Directions:

1. Cook sausage and drain.
2. Add cream cheese and cheddar cheese and mix together.
3. Remove crescent rolls from can and pinch them all together to make one big square.
4. Put mixture on square and spread evenly.
5. Roll all of it to make a log.
6. Freeze overnight.
7. Remove and slice into pinwheels and bake at 350 degrees for 15 minutes.

Ingredients:

2 pounds of hot sausage
2 packs of cream cheese
1 cup of shredded cheddar cheese
4 cans of crescent rolls

Easy Chili Mac

Contributed By: Pauline Hobbs

Ingredients:

1 cup dried elbow macaroni
1 lb ground beef
1 medium onion, diced
2 14.5 cans petite diced tomatoes
1 can Bushes chili hot beans with sauce
½ cup ketchup
2-3 tablespoons chili powder
2 teaspoons ground cumin
1 teaspoon garlic powder
1 teaspoon sugar
½ teaspoon paprika

Directions:

1. Cook macaroni according to package directions, drain.
2. Cook ground beef and diced onion until beef is browned and onions are soft, drain.
3. Combine all ingredients in a large stock pot and simmer for 20-30 minutes.
4. Serve with shredded cheddar cheese and sour cream.
5. Cornbread or Fritos are great sides with this chili. Enjoy!

Rick's Super Smokin' Ribs

Contributed By: Rick Hale

Directions:

1. For the grill or smoker (ideal), ceramic smokers are awesome and I personally own a Green Egg that I love for temperature control all day and juiciness it produces every time! I like baby back ribs but all will work– as many racks as will fit on your grill or smoker upright and in a rib rack.
2. Remove the membrane (I use a paper towel and knife to grab the corner and pull it off after rinsing them off)
3. If it won't come off, just gently score the bone side as lightly as you can to help it cook off somewhat as you cook.
4. Apply your favorite rub (apply the night before and refrigerate, but a minimum of an hour or two will work as well...rub it in good! I cut the full rack of ribs into manageable sizes...usually thirds, or 5-6 rib bones each.
5. Get the grill going as far in advance as necessary to lock into a temp just under 200 degrees... .170-185 is ideal. Stabilize to insure you stay "in the zone" – go ahead and soak your wood chips for an hour or more to insure they smoke the way you want them to and apply them to the coals directly just before putting the drip pan, rib rack and ribs in the smoker.
6. Remember, use a pan and rib rack to hold the ribs for stage one - stacked side by side in the rack and inside of a drip pan.
7. I vary the juice options in the drip pan- sometimes a can of beer, apple juice or cider....but my favorite is combo of peach nectar and pineapple juice. Put enough in the pan to sustain the first hour to hour and a half of cooking/smoking. If you choose to use a can of beer, grab three. Pour two in and drink the third one (or more) to enhance the experience on a hot summer day.
8. The **First Hour** plus is all about smoke and indirect heat. I move the ribs around a little if they are touching to expose all areas of the ribs to smoke after 40-45 minutes (half way in step one). Watch that temperature...keep it low and slow, and remember, "if you're lookin', you're NOT cookin'" ....let it go and relax.
9. The **Second Hour** – Carefully pull off the ribs- set up sheets of aluminum foil usually 12"-14" in length to wrap them in. Oversized package is even better to fully wrap and hold juices in for stage two! You can either buy special grilling aluminum foil (non-stick) or just spray the foil to

insure the ribs don't stick.

10. Put only one rib section in each foil sheet....non-stick side inside, and make a boat out of it before fully covering it capable of holding half a cup of your juice from the drip pan (mmmmm good!). You are creating your very own bed of juiciness for the smoked ribs to now cook in adding more tenderness. NOTE: keep the temp down- under 180 works best for me. Fully wrap each rib section and stack them on the grill surface. (throw out the rest of the juice and discard the drip pan once all wrapped up)

11. Let it go for an hour to hour and a half....note...if you like really tender, ridiculous fall off the bone ribs, this is the secret. The longer you go, the more tender, but harder to keep attached when you move onto the last hour!

12. The **Third to Fourth Hour** or longer (depending on time you have!) – I pull the foiled ribs off, let cool for a few minutes and then take them out of the aluminum foil bedding you lovingly gave them to steep in. Apply them to the grill for the final leg and finish!

13. I also toss a little Kielbasa or apple chicken sausage around them to smoke while on the last leg and a great compliment to the amazing ribs you just smoked up!

14. I typically let the grill get a little hotter in this phase to put some "bark or dark finish on them." 250-300 degrees, but be careful.

15. Grill for 30-45 minutes naked (sometimes if hot, the sauce will burn a little....some actually love that and a personal preference). Flip a few times once again for even cooking and to put the bite back in and firm them up a little.

16. Last step is to apply your favorite BBQ sauce (see Rick's Super Sauce) and flip a few more times for 20-30 minutes depending on temperature and the finish you are after (personal tastes)– find a large platter and carefully pull off your meat-extravaganza and amaze your friends. Let stand/cool a little- typically 5-10 minutes and serve it up.

17. Note, I like bbq sauce made by The Salt Lick (on line only or in Texas- from Austin), Sweet Baby Ray's and of course my own custom sauce - Rick's Super Sauce.

Rick's Super Sauce

vinegar based goodness!

Contributed By: Rick Hale

Directions:

1. Blend ingredients into cider vinegar slowly and simmer in a sauce pan for a half an hour or so....cool, jar it up and let it hang in fridge for a few hours to a few days...even months to maximize flavor!
2. Could also try adding a tablespoon of liquid smoke (hickory)... not tried it yet- let me know if it work out!
3. This sauce is good on everything, ribs, chicken, pork, shrimp........very distinctive and not one you'll find on the shelf at the grocery.

Ingredients:

½ Quart Apple Cider Vinegar
10 oz Ketchup
⅛ Cup Paprika
½ pound Brown Sugar
⅛ Cup Salt
1 T Black Pepper
1 T Cayenne Pepper (more if you like it more kickin!)
1 T Garlic Powder
⅛ Cup Worcestershire sauce
¼ Cup Lemon Juice

Slap Yo' Mama Butt Rubb

Contributed By: Rick Hale

Ingredients:

1 c. brown sugar
½ c. kosher salt
1 t. cinnamon
½ c. garlic salt (I'm partial to Lawry's)
1 t. coriander
½ c. smoked paprika
1 T. cayenne pepper (go easy on this if you're a spice weenie)
1 T. chili powder
1 T. freshly ground black pepper

Directions:

1. Blend ingredients and use as a rub for ribs, beef or meat of your choice.

Reuben Casserole

Contributed By: Sherri Levine

Directions:

1. In a 13×9-baking dish greased with butter, layer sauerkraut, sour cream & onion.
2. Crumble corned beef over kraut mixture.
3. Layer shredded Swiss cheese over corned beef.
4. Combine melted butter with rye bread crumbs, top casserole with bread crumb mixture.
5. Bake at 350 for 45-60 minutes. Serves 6-8.

Ingredients:

32 oz. jar sauerkraut, drained
1 cup sour cream
1 large onion, diced (1 cup)
1½ lb. corned beef, chipped & chopped
3 cups Swiss cheese, shredded
10 slices rye bread, made into crumbs
½ cup butter, melted

Maple Beans & Sausage

Contributed By: Deanna Morrell

Ingredients:

1 can (29 oz) pinto beans, rinsed
1 can (28 oz) baked beans
1 c chopped onion
⅓ c maple flavored pancake syrup
1 Tbsp dry mustard
8 oz turkey kielbasa, cut in ½ inch thick rounds (I frequently put more sausage than it calls for)
2 medium Golden Delicious apples, sliced

Directions:

1. Heat oven to 350 degrees.
2. Mix all ingredients in a shallow 2 qt baking dish until well blended.
3. Bake, uncovered, 55 to 60 min until apples are tender.

This recipe might not appeal to you on first glance but I promise that the flavors are so good together and a heart-warming meal on a cold and rainy day!

Desserts

There is no better way to conclude a great meal than with a sumptuous dessert.

Great Aunt Melba's Poundcake

Contributed by: Tammy Amsler

Ingredients:

2 sticks butter or margarine
2½ cups sugar
2 tsp. baking powder
6 eggs
1 tsp. lemon flavoring
½ pint whipping cream
3 cups sifted White Lily flour
¼ tsp. salt
1 tsp. vanilla flavoring

Directions:

1. Preheat oven to 325°.
2. Let ALL ingredients reach room temperature.
3. Cream butter and sugar.
4. Add eggs one at a time, beating well after each addition.
5. Sift together flour, salt, and baking powder.
6. Add to creamed mixture alternately with whipping cream.
7. Add flavorings and mix very well.
8. Pour into greased and floured tube pan.
9. Bake at 325° for 1 ½ hours.

Sour Cream Pound Cake

Contributed by: Heather Abramo

Directions:

1. Grease and flour a 10 inch tube pan.
2. Set oven at 350 degrees.
3. Sift flour, soda and ¼ tsp salt together.
4. Separate egg white from yolks.
5. Beat egg whites until foamy and add remaining ¼ tsp salt, beat until stiff peaks form.
6. Set aside.
7. Cream butter sugar and vanilla~add one egg yolk at a time beating well after each addition.
8. Add flour mixture alternately with sour cream.
9. Fold in beaten egg whites (with large spoon) until thoroughly mixed.
10. Pour into tube pan and bake 50 to 60 minutes.
11. Cake is done when it is firm to the touch on top.
12. Cool on hot pad for 5 to 10 minutes before turning onto plate.

Note: Do not beat the egg whites in - just fold gently until blended; this gives the cake volume. I serve with frosting or with fresh fruit, strawberries macerated in sugar are great (no water because the sugar makes it syrupy). Just mash strawberries and sugar together and let it sit while the cake bakes.

Ingredients:

3 cups sugar
2 sticks butter (softened at room temp)
6 eggs
3 cups sifted cake flour (plain)
1 8oz container of sour cream
½ tsp salt (divided)
¼ tsp baking soda
1 tsp vanilla

Snickerdoodles

Contributed by: Renee Tiller

Ingredients:

2¾ cups flour
1 tsp baking soda
2 eggs
½ cup shortening
1 tsp salt
1½ cups sugar
1 tsp vanilla
2 tsp cream of tartar
½ cup margarine

Directions:

1. Cream sugar, margarine, vanilla, soda, shortening, salt, cream of tartar and eggs.
2. Then add flour.
3. Roll in walnut size balls.
4. Roll in sugar/cinnamon mixture.
5. Bake 8-10 min at 400 degrees.

Japanese Fruit Pie

via Mary Kline and Nancy Singer

Contributed by: Rebecca Singer

Directions:

1. Beat eggs until stiff.
2. Add sugar and margarine, and stir.
3. Mix coconut, raisins and chopped pecans together.
4. Add coconut mixture to egg mixture.
5. Add vanilla and vinegar and stir.
6. Pour mixture into pie shells (may make 3 small or 2 larger pies).
7. Bake at 325 for 1 hour.

Ingredients:

4 eggs
2 cups sugar
2 sticks margarine
1 cup coconut
1 cup raisins
1 cup chopped pecans
2 teaspoons vanilla
2 teaspoons vinegar

Pumpkin Squares

Contributed by: Michelle Queen

Ingredients:

4 eggs
¼ cup vegetable oil
1 (18.25 oz) package yellow cake mix
½ t ground cinnamon
1 t vanilla extract
1 (15 oz) can solid pack pumpkin
1 (14 oz) can EAGLE BRAND® Sweetened Condensed Milk (NOT evaporated milk)
½ t salt

Directions:

1. Preheat oven to 350 (325 for glass dish).
2. Grease a 13x9 inch baking pan.
3. Reserve ½ cup dry cake mix.
4. In large mixing bowl; combine remaining cake mix, oil and 1 egg.
5. Beat until crumbly.
6. Stir in nuts if desired.
7. Press firmly on bottom of greased 13x9 inch baking pan.
8. In same bowl, combine ½ cup reserved cake mix and remaining ingredients.
9. Mix well.
10. Pour over prepared crust.
11. Bake for 50 minutes or until set.
12. Cool.
13. Cut into bars.
14. Store in a tightly covered container.

Grandma Schaeffer's Jumbo Chocolate Jumbo Cookies

Contributed by: Dana Schaeffer

Directions:

1. Combine sugar, shortening, cocoa and salt.
2. Add hot coffee. Cool to room temperature.
3. Add molasses and stir in flour, baking soda and vanilla. Mix thoroughly.
4. Refrigerate mixture overnight.
5. Roll out and cut out cookies.
6. Bake at 350 degrees for 6-7 minutes.
7. After cookies are completely cool, ice cookies with vanilla icing.

IMPORTANT TIP!!! WARNING!!! Keep the batter COLD while rolling it out or it become VERY sticky. Flour board and rolling pin well.

Ingredients:

1 Cup Brown Sugar Packed
⅔ Cup Shortening
½ Cup Cocoa
1 Cup Hot Coffee
½ Teaspoon Salt
1 Cup Molasses
3 Cups Flour
1 Teaspoon Baking Soda
1 Teaspoon Vanilla

Icing:

2 Cups Confectioner's Sugar
⅓ butter (melted)
1 teaspoon Vanilla
Add milk to desired consistency

Jewish Apple Cake

Lillian Retzger

Contributed By: Rebecca Singer

Ingredients:

4 apples
1 teaspoon cinnamon
3 cups sifted flour
2¼ cups + 2 teaspoons sugar
1½ teaspoon baking powder
4 eggs
1 cup oil
7 tablespoons orange juice
1 teaspoon vanilla

Directions:

1. Peel and chop 4 apples.
2. Sprinkle with 1 teaspoon cinnamon and 2 teaspoons sugar.
3. Set aside.
4. Grease a tube pan.
5. Mix the flour, 2¼ cups sugar, baking powder, eggs, oil, orange juice and vanilla together.
6. Pour half of the flour batter into the greased tube pan.
7. Sprinkle with ½ of the chopped apples.
8. Pour remaining batter on top of apples.
9. Sprinkle remaining apples on top.
10. Bake at 350 for 1½ hours or until toothpick comes out clean.

Toffee Fudge

Contributed By: Nancy Hayes

Directions:

1. Grease a 9" square pan with butter.
2. Stir sugar, marshmallow creme, cream and butter in a heavy 3 qt saucepan over medium heat until mixtures comes to a full boil.
3. Boil, stirring constantly, for 6 minutes.
4. Remove from heat and stir in chips until melted, then the toffee bars. (Note: It's possible that neither the chips nor the toffee bars will melt completely; that's fine.)
5. Pour into prepared pan and chill until firm.
6. Keep stored in the refrigerator.

It is really hard to get the toffee out of the pan once it is completely cooled. I recommend waiting until it's been chilled a couple of hours and then use a very sharp knife to cut into small squares and remove the squares from the pan. Definitely make the squares small as it is very sweet and you can't eat much at a time! Place in another container - if you stack the candy in layers, be sure to put wax paper or saran wrap between the layers. Store airtight in the refrigerator.

This is my favorite candy recipe because you don't have to use a candy thermometer, it is virtually impossible to mess up the recipe, and it's my favorite fudge ever. People rave about it when they eat it.

Ingredients:

1 lb light brown sugar
1.5 cups marshmallow creme (6 ozs) or marshmallow fluff (9.5 ozs)
¾ cup light cream
¼ cup butter
1 cup butterscotch chips (6 ozs)
5 Skor or Heath bars, about 1.25 ozs each - chopped coarse

St. Patrick's Day Cupcakes

because they are green!

Contributed By: Abby Hood

Ingredients:

1¾ cups all-purpose flour
1 4-serving side pkg. instant pistachio pudding mix
¾ cups chocolate chips (I round up to 1 cup sometimes!)
⅔ cups sugar
2½ tsp. baking powder
½ tsp. salt
2 beaten eggs
1¼ cups milk
½ cups cooking oil
1 tsp. vanilla extract
1 container of cream cheese frosting
green colored sugar/sprinkles (optional)

Directions:

1. Grease muffin cups or line with paper baking cups.
2. In large bowl, stir together flour, pudding mix, chocolate pieces, sugar, baking powder and salt.
3. In a small bowl, combine beaten eggs, milk, oil and vanilla.
4. Stir into flour mixture just until combined.
5. Fill muffin cups ⅔ full.
6. Bake in 375 oven for 18-20 minutes or until golden brown.
7. Cool on a wire rack.
8. Frost with cream cheese frosting and sprinkle with green sugar/sprinkles.

Quick Italian Cream Cake

Contributed By: Kathy Vaughn

Directions:

1. BEAT first 4 ingredients at medium speed with an electric mixer 2 minutes.
2. Stir in coconut and pecans.
3. Pour batter into 3 greased and floured 9" round cake pans.
4. BAKE AT 350 degrees for 5 to 17 minutes or until a wooded pick inserted in center comes out clean.
5. Cool in pans on wire racks 10 minutes.
6. Remove from pans and cool completely on wire racks.
7. Sprinkle layers evenly with rum, if desired; let stand 10 minutes.
8. BEAT cream cheese and butter at medium speed with an electric mixer until smooth.
9. Gradually add powdered sugar, beating until light and fluffy.
10. Stir in pecans and vanilla. (4 cups)
11. SPREAD frosting between layers and on top and sides of cake.
12. Chill 2 hours before slicing.

Ingredients:

1 (18.5 oz) pkg. white cake mix with pudding
3 large eggs
1¼ cups buttermilk
⅓ cup vegetable oil
1 (3½ oz) can flaked coconut
⅔ cup chopped pecans, toasted
3 T. rum (optional)

Cream Cheese Frosting
1 (8 oz) pkg. cream cheese, softened
½ cup butter, softened
1 (16 oz) pkg. powdered sugar
1 cup chopped pecans, toasted
2 tsp. vanilla extract

Butter 'Em Up Butter Glazed Apples

Contributed By: Jill Van Nuis

Ingredients:

2 T butter
1 qt washed, cored, sliced apples (4 medium)
½ c sugar or brown sugar
½ t cinnamon

Directions:

1. Melt butter in large skillet.
2. Add apples and sprinkle with sugar and cinnamon.
3. Cover skillet.
4. Cook over low heat for 10 minutes.
5. Remove cover.
6. Cook over medium heat, stirring frequently until apples are glazed, tender and slightly transparent.
7. Serve warm.

Can be a side dish or dessert. Great with vanilla ice cream! Works great as a bribe.

Chocolate Cake Cookies

Contributed By: Callie Ruffus

Directions:

1. In a large bowl with an electric mixer, cream the cream cheese and butter until smooth.
2. Beat in the egg.
3. Then, beat in the vanilla extract.
4. Beat in the cake mix.
5. Cover and refrigerate for 2 hours to firm up so batter can roll into balls.
6. When ready to bake, heat oven to 350°.
7. Roll chilled batter into tablespoon-sized balls and then roll in powdered sugar.
8. Place on ungreased cookie sheet 2 inches apart.
9. Bake for 10 to 12 minutes.
10. The cookies will remain kind of soft and gooey.
11. Cool completely on wire racks and sprinkle with more powdered sugar if necessary.

Ingredients:

1 (8 oz.) block cream cheese, room temperature
1 stick unsalted butter, room temperature
1 egg, room temperature
1 teaspoon vanilla extract
1 (18 oz.) box moist chocolate cake mix (I like Pillsbury brand, but use whatever cake mix you like best)
Powdered sugar for dusting

Pecan & Chocolate Chip Breakfast Cookies

Contributed By: Mary Pierce

Ingredients:

3 cups white whole wheat flour
1½ cups rolled oats
1½ teaspoon baking soda
1 teaspoon ground cinnamon
½ teaspoon salt
1½ sticks unsalted butter, softened
1¼ cup Sucanat sugar or brown sugar
1 tablespoon pure vanilla extract
6 large eggs
1 cups chopped pecans
1 cup mini chocolate chips

Directions:

1. Preheat oven to 350 degrees.
2. In a large bowl mix together the flour, oats, baking soda, cinnamon, and salt. Set aside.
3. In your mixer or using a hand mixer, cream together butter and sugar in a large bowl.
4. Add in vanilla extract and eggs one at a time.
5. Slowly add flour mixture in ½ cup at a time.
6. Stir in pecans and chocolate chips.
7. Using a ¼ cup, drop cookie dough onto lightly sprayed cookie sheet.
8. Using your hands, shape and slightly flatten the cookie dough down.
9. Bake for 11 - 13 minutes. *Mine cooked perfectly at 12 minutes. Don't overcook because these taste better a little chewy.
10. Let cool for 5 minutes on cookie sheet then move to wire rack to finish cooling.

Make Ahead Instructions
These cookies freeze perfectly. After they cool, wrap in plastic wrap, then place in large freezer bag and label. To thaw take out and place on the counter for ½ hour or so.

Coconut Cream Cake

Contributed by: Mandi Bagwell

Directions:

1. Preheat oven to 350 degrees F (175 degrees C).
2. Grease and flour a 9x13 inch pan.
3. Combine the cake mix, oil, eggs, sour cream and cream of coconut In a medium bowl.
4. Mix until well blended.
5. Spread evenly into the prepared pan.
6. Bake in the preheated oven until a toothpick inserted into the cake comes out clean , almost for 25 to 30 mins,.
7. Allow to cool.
8. Make the frosting while your cake cools.
9. Cream together cream cheese, the confectioners sugar, and milk in a medium bowl.
10. Stir in the vanilla.
11. Frost cooled cake then sprinkle with coconut.

Ingredients:

1 (18.25 ounce) package white cake mix

1 (8 ounce) container sour cream

¼ cup vegetable oil

3 eggs

1 (8 ounce) can coconut cream

1 (8 ounce) package cream cheese

1 (16 ounce) package confectioners' sugar

1 teaspoon vanilla extract

2 tablespoons milk

1 cup flaked coconut

Lynda's Hot Fudge Pie

Contributed by: Laura Miller Edwards

Ingredients:

5 T. flour
3 T. cocoa
1 cup sugar
3 eggs, separated
1 t. vanilla
1 stick butter
½ cup milk
Pie Crust - cooked

Directions:

1. Mix flour, cocoa, sugar in a large glass bowl.
2. Add milk and butter.
3. Melt cooking in the microwave 3-4 minutes, until thick.
4. Stir occasionally using a whisk.
5. Beat yellows of eggs and add to hot mixture slowly.
6. Cook 1 minute, stir.
7. Cook 1 additional minute, stir in vanilla, pour into pie crust.

Meringue:
8. Beat egg whites until stiff.
9. Fold in ¼ cup sugar.
10. Pile on top.
11. Bake at 450 degrees until golden brown (about 5 minutes).

Sugar Cream Pie

Contributed by: Denise Hutchinson

Directions:

1. Combine sugar, flour & nutmeg.
2. Heat cream and butter (do not boil).
3. Add to sugar, flour and nutmeg mixture slowly.
4. Add salt.
5. Pour into unbaked pie shell.
6. Sprinkle with another pinch of nutmeg on top.
7. Bake at 450 for 10 minutes then at 350 for 30 to 40 minutes or until set.

OPTIONAL: Add fresh blueberries and press each just under the surface.

Ingredients:

1½ cups sugar
6 T flour
pinch of nutmeg
2 cups heavy whipping cream
2 T butter
pinch of salt
1 unbaked 9 inch pie shell
(Fresh Blueberries optional)

Praline Pecans

Contributed By: Laura Miller Edwards

Ingredients:

1½ cups granulated sugar
¾ cup firmly packed brown sugar
½ cup butter
½ cup milk
2 T. corn syrup
5 cups toasted pecan halves

Directions:

1. Stir together first 5 ingredients in a heavy 3-qt saucepan.
2. Bring to a boil over medium heat, stirring constantly.
3. Boil, stirring constantly, 7-8 minutes, or until a candy thermometer registers 234 degrees.
4. Remove from heat, and vigorously stir in pecans.
5. Spoon pecan mixture onto wax paper, spreading in an even layer.
6. Let stand 20 minutes or until firm.
7. Break praline-coated pecans apart into pieces.
8. Store in an airtight container at room temperature up to 1 week.
9. Freeze in an airtight container or zip-top plastic freezer bag up to 1 month.

Blueberry Coffee Cake

Contributed by: Denise Hutchinson

Directions:

1. Beat margarine and cream cheese at medium speed until creamy.
2. Gradually add 1 cup sugar, beating well.
3. Add eggs; beat well.
4. Combine flour, baking powder and salt.
5. Stir into margarine mixture.
6. Stir in vanilla, fold in berries.
7. Pour batter into a 9 inch round cake pan coated with cooking spray.
8. Combine 2 tablespoons sugar and cinnamon, sprinkle over batter.
9. Bake at 350 for 1 hour.

Ingredients:

¼ cup margarine, softened
1 (8 oz) pkg cream cheese
1 c sugar
1 egg
1 c flour
1 tsp. baking powder
¼ tsp salt
1 tsp vanilla
2 cups fresh or frozen blueberries (unthawed)
2 Tbsp sugar
1 tsp ground cinnamon

Sugarless Peanut Butter Cookies

Contributed by: Denise Hutchinson

Ingredients:

1¼ cups flour
1 egg
1½ tsp baking powder
1 Tbsp liquid sweetener
½ cup creamy peanut butter
¼ tsp salt
¼ cup water
1 cup vegetable oil

Directions:

1. Mix all ingredients together.
2. Shape into balls and place on ungreased cookie sheet.
3. Press with fork before baking.
4. Bake at 375 for 12 to 15 minutes.

Makes 22 cookies.

Monkey Bread

Contributed by: Denise Hutchinson

Directions:

1. Mix sugar and cinnamon together.
2. Roll quartered biscuits in sugar and cinnamon mixture.
3. Place nuts in the bottom of a bundt pan.
4. Place biscuits in pan on top of nuts.
5. Boil together 1 tsp cinn, 1¼ sticks butter, 1 tsp vanilla and 1 cup sugar.
6. Pour over biscuits.
7. Bake 350 for 35 minutes.
8. Cool for a few minutes then turn out of pan.

Ingredients:

4 cans biscuits, quartered
⅔ cup sugar
1 T cinnamon
Walnuts or pecans, chopped
1 tsp cinnamon
1¼ sticks butter
1 tsp vanilla
1 cup sugar

Whipping Cream Pound Cake

Contributed by: Mandi Bagwell

Ingredients:

3 sticks butter
3 cups sugar
6 eggs
3 cups cake flour
½ pt. whipping cream (do not whip)
2 tsp. vanilla

Directions:

1. Make sure all ingredients are room temperature.
2. Cream together, butter and sugar.
3. Add eggs one at a time and beat well after each addition.
4. Add flour and whipping cream alternately to first mixture.
5. Beat well.
6. Add vanilla and mix well.
7. Grease and flour bundt cake pan.
8. Put in a cold oven and bake at 325 degrees for 1 hour and 15 minutes.

Crockpot Christmas Mix

Contributed by: Prissy Dixon

Directions:

1. Layer all ingredients in a large crockpot (starting with peanuts).
2. Turn the pot on low, cover with lid, and leave sitting for 2 hours.
3. Then, remove lid and stir to combine.
4. Replace lid and leave sitting for another 30 minutes.
5. Stir again and then spoon mixture on to wax paper or non-stick aluminum foil.
6. Allow to harden for at least 1 hour.

Enjoy!

Ingredients:

16 oz. unsalted peanuts
16 oz. salted peanuts
12 oz. semi-sweet chocolate chips
12 oz. milk chocolate chips
20 oz. peanut butter chips
2 lbs. white almond bark or vanilla candy coating

Banana Nut Bread

Contributed by: Leigh Ann Vega

Ingredients:

⅓ cup veg. oil
2½ ripe bananas
½ tsp. vanilla
3 eggs
2⅓ cups of Bisquick
1 cup of sugar
½ cup of chopped nuts
1 8 oz. bar of cream cheese

Directions:

1. Combine all ingredients and mix well.
2. Bake in loaf pan covered with foil for 45 minutes at 350 degrees.
3. Remove foil and bake for additional 15 minutes.

Momma's Original Pineapple Cake

Contributed by: Leigh Ann Vega

Directions:

1. Combine all of the ingredients and mix well.
2. Place in cake pan.
3. Bake @ 350 for 25 to 30 minutes

FROSTING
4. Combine frosting ingredients in mixing bowl.
5. Use mixer to blend.
6. Cool cake and frost.

Ingredients:

1 box of pineapple supreme cake mix
4 eggs
11 oz. can of mandarin orange drained (reserve 10 for garnish)
1½ cup of oil
1 small can of crushed pineapple drained

FROSTING
15 oz can crushed pineapple drained (reserve a small amount for garnish)
2- 3½ oz of French vanilla pudding
12 oz cool whip
11 oz can of mandarin oranges drained

Fruit Cake

Contributed by: Leigh Ann Vega

Ingredients:

1 butter cake mix
Fruit(s) of your choice

FROSTING
½ cup confectioner's sugar
½ cup of granulated sugar
8 oz cream cheese softened
12 oz cool whip

Directions:

1. Prepare cake mix as per directions.
2. Bake cake in cake pan, making two layers.
3. Allow to cool.
4. Place frosting ingredients in mixing bowl.
5. Mix with mixer.
6. Frost each layer then top with desired fruit.

Blueberry Pie

Contributed by: Mandi Bagwell

Directions:

CRUST:
1. Mix butter and flour by hand until it doesn't stick to hands. You may have to add up to ¼ cup more flour.
2. Press into 9 inch pie pan.
3. Flute sides and cut with fork.
4. Bake at 350 degrees for 20 minutes.

FILLING:
5. Whip cream cheese and add sugar; beat.
6. Add ½ tub of Cool Whip.
7. Pour into cooled pie shell and top with blueberry filling.

Ingredients:

1 cup flour
1 stick butter
(bought crust works great)

½ cup confectioners sugar
1 tsp. vanilla
1 can blueberry pie filling
(chilled)
12 oz. soft cream cheese
Cool Whip (small bowl)

Famous Hazelnut Cookies

Contributed by: Patti Loveless

Ingredients:

1¼ cups Self-Rising Flour, Sift &
Measure
½ cup White Sugar
½ cup Butter, Softened
½ cup Brown Sugar
½ cup Nutella (Hazelnut
Spread)
1 Egg
1 tsp Vanilla Extract
¾ cup Pecans, Chopped

Directions:

1. Preheat oven to 375°
2. In a medium bowl, using an electric mixer, cream together the butter, Nutella, white sugar and brown sugar for several minutes, until completely combined.
3. Add the egg and vanilla and mix until smooth, approximately 1 minute.
4. With a wooden utensil, fold in the flour until just combined.
5. Stir in nuts (can use any nut you like, pecans are a family favorite)
6. Line or grease a cookie sheet.
7. Spoon cookie mix on sheet with a tablespoon 4 inches apart.
8. Flatten the cookie dough with a fork.
9. Bake at 350° for 10-12 minutes or until edges are golden brown.
10. Transfer cookies with a metal spatula to a cooling rack.
11. Cool completely.

Quick & Easy Fruity Cake Dessert

Contributed by: Patti Loveless

Directions:

1. In medium frying pan, melt ¼ cup of butter.
2. Dump in pie filling (or any canned fruit mostly drained).
3. Cover with ½ to ¾ box of cake mix.
4. Cut up remaining butter and place on top.
5. Cover and cook until butter is melted and pie filling is bubbling.
6. Reduce heat, remove lid and cook until cake mix is fully cooked into filling.
7. Serve hot with a scoop of ice cream.

Ingredients:

1 Can Fruit Pie Filling, any flavor
1 Box Cake Mix, any kind
½ Cup Butter
½ Cup Chopped Nuts, optional

Pineapple Casserole

Contributed by: Rachel Konieczny

Ingredients:

1 cup sugar
6 tablespoons all-purpose flour
2 cups grated sharp cheddar cheese
2 (20-ounce) cans pineapple chunks or tidbits, drained
6 tablespoons pineapple juice reserved
1 cup Ritz cracker crumbs
8 tablespoons (1 stick of butter) melted plus extra for greasing the pan
Red and Green grapes, halved

Directions:

1. Preheat oven to 350 degrees F.
2. Grease a medium-size casserole dish with butter.
3. In a large bowl, stir together the sugar and flour.
4. Gradually stir in the cheese.
5. Add the drained pineapple chunks or tidbits, and stir until ingredients are well combined.
6. Pour the mixture into the prepared casserole dish.
7. In another medium bowl, combine the Ritz cracker crumbs, melted butter and reserved pineapple juice, stirring with a rubber spatula until evenly blended.
8. Spread crumb mixture on top of pineapple mixture.
9. Bake for 25 to 30 minutes or until golden brown.
10. Goes wonderful with holiday ham or over ice cream.

New York Cheesecake

Contributed by: Marna Friedman

Directions:

1. Butter the inside of a 10-inch spring form pan.
2. Wrap the sides of the springform pan with aluminum foil making sure it securely covers the pan, to prevent water seeping in when you place the cheesecake in a water bath to bake.
3. Preheat the oven to 300.
4. Using an electric mixer, and large bowl, beat the eggs with the sour cream until well blended.
5. In a separate, medium-sized bowl, beat the cream cheese with the butter until smooth and creamy.
6. Add cream cheese mixture to egg-sour cream mixture and beat until smooth.
7. Add the sugar (or Splenda), cornstarch, vanilla, lemon juice, and beat thoroughly, about 2 minutes.
8. Pour into the buttered springform pan and place in a roasting pan large enough to prevent the sides from touching.
9. Place in the oven and carefully pour in enough very hot tap water to reach halfway up the sides of the springform pan (I use my Keurig for hot water with no coffee).
10. Bake for 2 hours, 15 minutes, or until the cake is very lightly colored and a knife inserted in the center emerges clean.
11. Remove from the water bath and carefully peel the aluminum foil from around the pan.
12. Let stand at room temperature until completely cool, about 4 hours.
13. Refrigerate, covered, until well chilled.
14. Top with strawberries and serve with whipped cream.

Ingredients:

2 cups (one pint) sour cream, room temperature
4 8-ounce packages cream cheese, room temperature
8 tablespoons (one stick) unsalted butter, room temperature
1½ cups sugar or Splenda
2 tablespoons cornstarch
1½ teaspoons vanilla extract or 1 teaspoon vanilla bean paste
1 teaspoon fresh lemon juice

Raisin Challah Bread Pudding

Contributed by: Marna Friedman

Ingredients:

1½ lb unsliced Raisin Challah
(day old)
¼ lb. butter, melted
8 oz. Raisins
Zest of 1 lemon

PUDDING:
1½ qt. milk
6 eggs
3 egg yolks
12 oz. sugar
1 Vanilla Bean
1 T cinnamon/sugar mix

Directions:

1. Butter a muffin pan.
2. Preheat over to 325.
3. Cut bread into 1 inch cubes and place on cookie sheet.
4. Drizzle melted butter over bread.
5. "Toast" bread in oven until toasted on both sides.
6. Remove from oven and allow to cool.
7. Boil milk, 6 oz. sugar, vanilla bean and lemon zest.
8. Whip eggs with the 6 oz. sugar.
9. Slowly add milk mixture, while whisking and combine remainder of ingredients.
10. Place filling in muffin pan, sprinkling with cinnamon sugar.
11. Set muffin pan in a "water bath".
12. Bake in oven at 325 for 40 minutes.

Can serve with vanilla sauce or vanilla ice cream.

Awesome Almond Bars

Contributed by: Beth Haigh

Directions:

1. Melt coconut oil in tempered glass (Pyrex) liquid measuring cup seated in hot water bath (bowl on counter) or warm up oven for a short time and sit inside.
2. Stir occasionally until melted.
3. Place almonds in food processor and run until almonds are a meal.
4. Scrape sides with spatula.
5. Add additional almond meal, flax meal, salt, stevia, cinnamon & protein powder in food processor.
6. Run food processor until well mixed.
7. Scrape sides with spatula again.
8. Once coconut oil in liquid state, add coconut oil to food processor along with raw almond butter and vanilla extract.
9. Pulse until ingredients form a coarse paste.
10. Press mixture into an parchment paper-lined 7"x5" or 8"x8" baking dish.
11. Chill in refrigerator until mixture hardens...at least 1 hour or overnight.
12. Remove from refrigerator, cut into bars and serve. These need to be kept chilled. Good to keep around for quick grab-and-go breakfasts or snacks.

Note: No-bake, high-protein, high-fiber bars. Easy to make and the kids can help. Can grind flaxseed into meal with a coffee/herb grinder...use a different one than you use for coffee. Don't purchase pre-ground flaxmeal because flax loses its potency and begins to go rancid as soon as mealed. Read the vanilla extract label to make sure there is no added sugar.

Ingredients:

2.5 cups organic raw almonds
½ cup organic almond meal/flour
½ cup freshly ground organic flaxseed meal
¾ tsp ground Himalayan salt
¾ tsp powder stevia
¾ tsp organic ground cinnamon
2 scoops chocolate-flavored organic cold-processed protein powder
½ cup organic, cold-pressed extra-virgin coconut oil
½ cup raw almond butter
1 Tbsp organic pure vanilla extract

Aunt Helen's Ruggelach

Contributed by: Marna Friedman

Ingredients:

½ lb butter (2 sticks)
¼ cup sugar or Splenda
½ lb cream cheese
3 eggs
2 T baking powder
4 cups sifted flour

FILLING:
2 T cinnamon
2 cups sugar or Splenda
Coconut, Chopped Walnuts,
Chocolate Chips

Or use Strawberry Jam for
filling with cinnamon & sugar

Directions:

1. Cream butter, sugar and cream cheese in electric mixer.
2. Add baking powder.
3. Add flour with dough hook.
4. Refrigerate overnight.

FILLING:
5. Flour surface.
6. Separate dough into 4 pieces.
7. Roll each piece into long strips about 4" wide by about 24" wide.
8. Spread filling mix all along the strip.
9. Roll 3 times.
10. Cut off any excess dough.
11. Slice into 1 inch slices.
12. Place on baking sheet and bake 14 minutes or until lightly browned.

Peach Cake

Contributed by: Kerry Barr

Directions:

1. Mix all CAKE ingredients and spread onto greased & floured cookie sheet - bake at 350 about 20-25 mins (check often).
2. Combine cream cheese, vanilla instant pudding and milk. Beat well until thickens.
3. Spread on top of cooled cake.
4. Drain 1½ lg cans sliced or diced peaches (or fruit of choice) - RESERVE LIQUID.
5. Thicken peach liquid with corn starch and mix with peaches; cool - spread on top of cream cheese topping (Canned pie filled can be used instead of canned fruit)
6. Spread Cool Whip or whipped cream over fruit topping

Ingredients:

CAKE
1 pkg yellow cake mix
1 cup water
1 cup oil
2 eggs
½ pkg instant vanilla pudding

TOPPING
8 oz cream cheese
1½ pkgs vanilla instant pudding
1½ cup milk

FRUIT
Drain 1½ lg cans sliced or diced peaches (or fruit of choice) - RESERVE LIQUID

Pudding Chocolate Chunk Cookies

Contributed by: Callie Ruffus

Ingredients:

1 cup unsalted butter, softened
¾ cup packed brown sugar
¼ cup sugar
1 (3.4 oz.) box Jell-O Vanilla instant pudding mix (can use chocolate too, but haven't tried that yet)
1 teaspoon vanilla extract
2 eggs, room temperature
1 teaspoon baking soda
2¼ cups flour (I use all-purpose flour)
1 (12 oz.) package semi-sweet chocolate chunks (or chips)

Directions:

1. Heat oven to 375°.
2. Beat butter, brown sugar, regular sugar, pudding mix, and vanilla with mixer until well blended.
3. Add eggs and baking soda; mix well.
4. Gradually beat in flour.
5. Stir in chocolate chunks.
6. Drop teaspoonfuls of dough 2 inches apart onto baking sheets.
7. Bake 8 to 10 minutes or until golden brown.
8. Cool 3 minutes on baking sheets and then completely on wire racks.

Bar variation: Make dough as above. Spread dough onto bottom of 13 x 9-inch pan sprayed with cooking spray. Bake at same temperature for 20 to 25 minutes or until golden brown.

Sugar Cookies

Contributed by: Callie Ruffus

Directions:

1. In large mixing bowl, combine sugar, butter, egg, whipping cream, and vanilla.
2. Beat at medium speed with mixer until light and fluffy.
3. Add flour, baking powder, and salt.
4. Beat at low speed until soft dough forms.
5. Cover with plastic wrap and chill 1 to 2 hours until firm.
6. Heat oven to 400°.
7. On floured surface, roll dough to ¼-inch thickness.
8. Cut cookies into desired shapes using cookie cutters.
9. Place shapes 2 inches apart on ungreased cookie sheets.
10. Bake for 4 to 6 minutes or until edges are light golden brown.
11. Cool on cookie sheets for 5 minutes and then transfer and cool completely on wire racks.
12. Decorate with frosting/icing, if desired.

Ingredients:

1 cup sugar
¾ cup unsalted butter, softened
1 egg, room temperature
3 tablespoons whipping cream
1 teaspoon vanilla extract
3 cups flour
1½ teaspoons baking powder
½ teaspoon salt

Hidden Mint Cookies

Contributed by: Callie Ruffus

Ingredients:

Sugar cookie dough (any recipe you like, see recipe on previous page)
1 (14 oz.) package Andes candies, chopped (or buy a bag already chopped pieces)

Directions:

1. Heat oven to 375°.
2. Roll out cookie dough and cut to size you want.
3. Place the cookies on ungreased baking sheets 2 to 3 inches apart.
4. Place Andes candy pieces in middle of cookie and fold over one side, pinch ends together or use fork.
5. Bake for 10 minutes or until edges are a light golden brown.
6. Let cool on pan for 5 minutes and then transfer to cool completely on wire rack.

Oreo Truffles

Contributed by: Callie Ruffus

Directions:

1. Mix cream cheese and 3 cups cookie crumbs until well blended (I use my mixer to make it easy).
2. Shape mixture into 1-inch balls.
3. Dip the balls in melted chocolate.
4. Place on waxed paper-covered baking sheet. Sprinkle tops with remaining cookie crumbs.
5. Refrigerate 1 hour or until firm (can be put in freezer for quicker time, but don't forget them in there!).
6. Store tightly in the refrigerator.

Ingredients:

1 (8 oz.) package cream cheese, softened

1 (1 lb. 2 oz.) package Oreo cookies, finely crushed and divided (3 cups, and then whatever is left)

2 (8 squares each) packages Baker's semi-sweet chocolate, melted (I use a small saucepan and melt one package at a time)

Cheesecake

Contributed by: Kerry Barr

Ingredients:

CRUST
1½ pkgs graham crackers - crushed
1 stick butter - melted

CHEESE CAKE - basic
4 8 oz pkgs cream cheese - softened
1 Cup sour cream - room temp
1½ Cups sugar
4 eggs - room temp
1 tsp vanilla

Directions:

1. CRUST - Mix ingredients together and press onto bottom and up sides of spring form pan.

FILLING:
2. Mix all above together - pour into prepared crust (If desired, add dollops of raspberry jelly to top of cake before baking and gently swirl through)
3. Bake at 350 degrees for 1 hour.
4. Turn off oven and leave cake in oven for 1 addition al hour. DO NOT OPEN OVEN DOOR

PUMPKIN VARIATION:
Mix cheese cake as above - add:
1 small can pumpkin
1 egg - room temp (for total of 5 eggs)
1 TBSP pumpkin pie spice

Mix well and bake as above

TOPPING:
1 cup light brown sugar
1 cup flour
½ cup chopped pecans
1 stick (approx) melted butter

Mix together and place on top.

Persimmon Pudding

Contributed by: Denise Hutchinson

Directions:

1. Mix all ingredients together and refrigerate.
2. Serve with Cool Whip
3. If desired, mix all ingredients together and form into a log.
4. Roll log in additional graham cracker crumbs and wrap in wax paper.
5. Refrigerate overnight.
6. Slice log into pieces and serve with cool whip.

Ingredients:

1 cup persimmon pulp

1 cup sugar or ½ c Splenda sugar blend

½ cup peanuts crushed

12 large marshmallows, cut up (or equivalent in small marshmallows)

18 Graham cracker squares crushed

Speedy Caramel Frosting

Contributed by: Denise Hutchinson

Ingredients:

½ cup butter
1 cup brown sugar
¼ tsp salt
¼ cup milk
2 to 2½ cup sifted powdered sugar
1 tsp vanilla
1 T. white corn syrup

Directions:

1. Melt butter in saucepan, stir in brown sugar and salt.
2. Cook and stir over low heat for 2 minutes.
3. Add milk, continue stirring until boiling.
4. Remove from heat and pour into a mixing bowl.
5. Add vanilla and corn syrup.
6. While beating with mixer...gradually add powdered sugar.
7. Be sure you have the cake ready to be iced. This recipe works best if you work quickly and ice cake while icing is warm.
8. If you are icing a one layer cake it is easier to pour this on while icing is still warm.

Peanut Butter Fudge

Contributed by: Denise Hutchinson

Directions:

1. Boil sugar, cream and corn syrup to soft boil stage.
2. Add butter, peanut butter and vanilla.
3. Cool slightly, then beat until creamy.
4. Pour into buttered 8 x 8 pan, let set.
5. Cut into squares and store in air tight container.
6. Can freeze.

Ingredients:

2 cups sugar (1 white, 1 brown)
¾ cup cream or half and half
2 T. white corn syrup
2 T. butter
2 Heaping Tablespoons peanut butter (un-homogenized works best)
1 tsp. vanilla

Miracle Whip Cake

Contributed by: Denise Hutchinson

Ingredients:

1 cup sugar
4 tsp cocoa (stir into sugar)
1 cup hot water
2 tsp baking soda (dissolved in hot water)
1 cup Miracle Whip
2 cups cake flour

Directions:

1. After mixing sugar & cocoa, add miracle whip and mix well.
2. Then, stir in flour.
3. Last, add water/baking soda mixture gradually.
4. Bake in buttered 9 x 12 pan at 350 for 25 minutes (or until toothpick comes out clean)

Chocolate Cobbler

Contributed by: Jo Cunningham

Directions:

1. Preheat oven to 350 degrees.
2. First stir together the flour, baking powder, salt, 3 tablespoons of the cocoa, and ¾ cup of the white sugar.
3. Reserve the remaining cocoa and sugar.
4. Stir in the milk, melted butter, and vanilla to the flour mixture.
5. Mix until smooth.
6. Pour the mixture into an ungreased 8-inch baking dish. I prefer my small oval Corning Ware glass dish.
7. In a separate small bowl, mix the remaining white sugar (it should be ½ cup), the brown sugar, and remaining 4 tablespoons of cocoa. Sprinkle this mixture evenly over the batter.
8. Pour the hot tap water over all. DO NOT STIR!
9. Bake for about 40 minutes or until the center is set.
10. Let stand for a few minutes if you can hold yourself back.
11. Serve with homemade ice cream using the gooey sauce to spoon over all.

Ingredients:

1 cup All-purpose Flour
2 teaspoons Baking Powder
¼ teaspoons Salt
7 Tablespoons Cocoa Powder, Divided
1-¼ cup Sugar, Divided
½ cups Milk
⅓ cups Melted Butter
1-½ teaspoon Vanilla Extract
½ cups Light Brown Sugar, Packed
1-½ cup Hot Tap Water

Magic Marshmallow Crescent Puffs

These great little magic puffs are great served right out of the oven & melt in your mouth! The marshmallow completely disappears and the inside of the "puff" is covered in butter, cinnamon & marshmallow. Always a hit on Christmas morning!

Contributed by: Dianne Piecuch

Ingredients:

Rolls:
¼ cup granulated sugar
2 Tablespoons all-purpose flour
1 teaspoon ground cinnamon
2 cans Pillsbury refrigerated crescent dinner rolls
16 large marshmallows
¼ cup butter or margarine, melted

Glaze:
½ cup powdered sugar
½ teaspoon vanilla
2 to 3 teaspoons milk
¼ cup chopped nuts (if desired)

Directions:

1. Heat oven to 375 degrees.
2. Spray 16 medium muffin cups with no-stick cooking spray. In small bowl, mix granulated sugar, flour and cinnamon.
3. Separate dough into 16 triangles.
4. For each roll, dip 1 marshmallow into melted butter.
5. Roll in sugar mixture.
6. Place marshmallow on shortest side of triangle.
7. Roll up, starting at shortest side and rolling to opposite point.
8. Completely cover marshmallow with dough, firmly pinch edges to seal.
9. Dip 1 end in remaining butter; place butter side down in muffin cup.
10. Bake 12-15 minutes or until golden brown. (Place foil or cookie sheet on rack below muffin cups to guard against spills.)
11. Cool in pan 1 minute.
12. Remove rolls from muffin cups, place on cooling racks set over waxed paper.
13. In small bowl, mix powdered sugar, vanilla & enough milk for desired drizzling consistency.
14. Drizzle glad over warm rolls.
15. Sprinkle with nuts.
16. Serve warm (although they can be lightly microwaved to warm them up the next day)!

Egg Nog Pumpkin Pie

Contributed by: Bill Celler

Directions:

1. Beat together first 5 ingredients, then blend in pumpkin.
2. Pour into deep-dish crust.
3. Bake at 450° for 10 minutes, then at 350° for 45 minutes (or until done).
4. Top off with cinnamon or nutmeg and have at it!

Ingredients:

1 ½ cups egg nog
16 oz pumpkin filling
2 eggs
8-9" deep dish pie crust
½ cup sugar
1 ½ tsps cinnamon
½ tsp salt

Black Bottom Cupcakes

Contributed by: Dianne Piecuch

Ingredients:

Muffins:
1 cup sugar
1½ cup all-purpose flour
½ teaspoon salt
½ cup cocoa
1 cup water
1 Tablespoon white vinegar
1 teaspoon baking soda

Filling:
1 8 oz package of cream cheese (the real stuff...not low fat)
1 egg
⅓ cup sugar
⅛ teaspoon salt
1 6 oz package semi-sweet chocolate chips

Directions:

1. Preheat oven to 350 degrees.
2. ((For best results, put aluminum foil cupcake cups directly on a cookie sheet rather than using a muffin pan.))
3. Mix muffin ingredients together and fill muffin cups ⅓ full. Put 1 Tablespoon of filling on top of each. Bake at 350 degrees for 25 minutes.

Peanut Butter Balls

Contributed by: Teena Regan

Directions:

1. Mix 2 ingredients together until substance is dry and pliable.
2. Roll into one inch balls and freeze for 2 hours or overnight if preferred.
3. Melt 8 pack bar of chocolate in microwave for 2 minutes.
4. Remove Peanut Butter Balls from fridge and dip in chocolate.
5. Roll around and remove with a spoon and place on wax paper.
6. Refrigerate until ready to eat.

Ingredients:

2 cups of smooth peanut butter
3 cups of confectioner sugar (some peanut butters are more oily than others so this amount could vary)
chocolate bar with paraffin wax

Christmas Holly Leaf Cookies

Contributed by: Rachel Konieczny

Ingredients:

1 stick of butter
40 large marshmallows
1 tablespoon of Vanilla
Green food coloring (to make deep green color)
4 cups of corn flakes
Red Hots

Directions:

1. Melt butter and marshmallows in a large saucepan.
2. Remove from heat and quickly mix in the vanilla and green food coloring until you have a deep green color.
3. Mix in the corn flakes and stir until evenly coated.
4. Drop onto cookie sheets or waxed paper and dot with red hot.
5. Makes about 28 cookies.

Chocolate Eclair Cake

Contributed by: Callie Ruffus

Directions:

1. Grease 13x9 dish with butter.
2. Line with whole graham crackers.
3. Mix pudding and milk together.
4. Beat 2 minutes and fold in cool whip.
5. Pour a good layer over the graham crackers, then add another layer of graham crackers and continue to alternate ending with graham crackers on top.
6. Add sugar, salt, cocoa and milk to a pan and bring to a boil.
7. Let cook 1 minute.
8. Remove from heat and add butter and vanilla.
9. Beat until smooth and thick enough to spread.
10. Pour over the top of graham crackers.

Ingredients:

Filling:
1- 9-11oz cool whip
1 box graham crackers
2- 3 ¾ oz box of french vanilla instant pudding
3 cups milk

Frosting:
1 cup granulated sugar
⅛ tsp salt
⅓ cup chocolate cocoa
¼ cup milk
¼ cup butter
1 tsp vanilla

Cheese Danish

This is a must have breakfast snack with coffee on camping trips!

Contributed by: Jeff VanHuss

Ingredients:

3 Cans Crescent Rolls
2 8 oz. packages Cream Cheese (Reduced Fat may be used)
¾ Cup of Sugar (I use an equal amount of Splenda and it works great)
1 Egg Yolk
1 Teaspoon Lemon Juice
½ Teaspoon Vanilla
1 Egg White, beaten
Powdered Sugar for topping

Directions:

1. Spread 1½ cans of the crescent rolls in the bottom of a jelly roll pan sprayed with a nonstick cooking spray. Mix together the cream cheese, egg yolk, sugar, lemon juice and vanilla.
2. A small amount of milk, just about a tablespoon, can be added here if mixture will not spread well.
3. Spread on top of the rolls.
4. Spread the remaining rolls on top of the cheese mixture and brush with egg white.
5. Bake at 350 for 20 - 25 minutes - should be lightly browned.
6. Cool completely and sprinkle with powdered sugar. The recipe can easily be doubled if feeding a larger crowd!
7. Cut into squares and keep for several days in a covered plastic container.

Christine's Fresh Strawberry & Almond Cake

Contributed by: Donna Carver

Directions:

1. Bake 2 layers of cake using directions on box.
2. Let cool completely then using a long knife and pancake flipper, cut each of the 2 layers horizontally making 4 layers in total.
3. If the strawberries and lemons have been frozen a head of time, they need to be completely thawed before using.
4. In a small bowl, macerate strawberries by adding lemon juice and zest.
5. Let it set for 20 minutes.
6. Then, mix strawberry Jello (dry) and vanilla pudding mix (dry) to strawberries and blend.
7. Fold in sliced almonds.
8. Add Cool Whip.
9. Use about ½ cup of topping mixture between each layer of the cake.
10. Use the rest on the top and sides of the cake.
11. Refrigerate until served.

Ingredients:

1 box Duncan Hines Moist Deluxe Classic White Cake mix
1½ cups fresh strawberries, sliced
2 lemons (juice and zest)
2 tubs (8 oz. each) Kraft Cool Whip lite whipped topping
1 small box strawberry Jello (sugar free)
2 small boxes (or l large box) instant Jello vanilla pudding (sugar free and fat free)
1 cup sliced almonds

Chewies

Contributed by: Nancy Hayes

Ingredients:

1 c light brown sugar
1 c dark brown sugar
2 eggs
1 T vanilla
2 sticks of butter, melted
2 c self rising flour
2 c chopped pecans

Directions:

1. Butter an 8x8 or 9x9 pan depending on your preference. Melt the butter.
2. Stir in the first 4 ingredients well and then mix in the rest.
3. Cover the pan lightly with aluminum foil if your oven tends to burn things.
4. Bake at 350 degrees for 30-35 min.
5. The secret to great Chewies is to take them out a tiny bit before you think they are done to preserve the chewiness.
6. If a toothpick to the middle comes out with just a little bit on it but the sides are firm, they are probably ready to come out. They firm up some after they come out.

Christine's Orange Pecan Muffins

Contributed by: Donna Carver

Directions:

1. Mix flour, soda, salt, baking powder in a mixing bowl.
2. In a separate bowl, mix sugar, melted butter or oil, zest and beaten egg.
3. Combine ingredients.
4. Grease and flour muffin tin.
5. Fill muffin tin with mixture.
6. Before baking, put pecan halves and brown sugar on top of each muffin.
7. Bake at 350 degree preheated oven.
8. Check for doneness by using the toothpick test. That is, insert toothpick in center of muffin. If the toothpick comes out clean, the muffin is done. If not, cook longer and then recheck for doneness.

Ingredients:

1¾ cups all purpose flour
1 teaspoon baking soda
1 teaspoon salt
2 teaspoons baking powder
¾ cup sugar
1 stick butter or ½ cup vegetable oil
¾ cup freshly squeezed orange juice
1 egg (beaten)
1 tablespoon zest (finely grated orange rind)

Topping:
12 pecan halves
6 teaspoons brown sugar

Chocolate Zucchini Cake

Contributed by: Deanna Morrell

Ingredients:

½ c of soft butter
4 tbsp. cocoa
½ c of vegetable oil
2 whole eggs
½ tsp of baking powder
1¾ c of sugar
½ tsp of cinnamon
½ tsp of ground cloves
1 tsp of vanilla
2 c of diced zucchini (not shredded)
½ c of sour milk*
¼ c of chocolate chips
2 ½ c of flour

Directions:

1. Cream butter, oil & sugar.
2. Add eggs, vanilla and milk. Beat with mixer until well blended.
3. Mix together dry ingredients and add to creamed mixture and mix gradually. Beat well.
4. Stir in zucchini by hand.
5. Spoon batter into greased & floured 9x12x2 pan. Sprinkle top with chocolate chips.
6. Bake at 325 for 40-45 minutes.
7. No frosting is needed for this very moist cake.
8. When cool, a dusting of powder sugar is an option.

To sour milk: Add 1 tsp of lemon juice to ½ c of whole milk. Let stand 5 minutes and then use in recipe

Pumpkin Ice Cream Pie

Contributed by: Deanna Morrell

Directions:

1. Spoon ice cream into pie crust.
2. Freeze while making the pumpkin mix.
3. Combine all ingredients except whipping cream. Whip cream until stiff peaks form.
4. Gently fold in pumpkin mixture.
5. Spread over the ice cream.
6. Cover and \freeze at least 8 hours (24 hours is better).
7. Serve the pie frozen.

Ingredients:

1 pint of French vanilla ice cream softened
1 baked 9" graham cracker pie crust
1 cup of canned pumpkin
¾ c of sugar
½ tsp of ground ginger
½ tsp of ground cinnamon
½ tsp of salt
¼ tsp of freshly grated nutmeg (or ½ tsp of ground nutmeg)
1 c of whipping cream

Mississippi Mud Cake

Contributed by: Deanna Morrell

Ingredients:

1 c of chopped pecans
½ c unsweet cocoa
1 c of butter
4 large eggs
1 4 oz semi-sweet chocolate baking bar chopped
1 tsp vanilla
2 c of sugar
¾ tsp salt
1½ c of flour
1 (10.5) bag of miniature marshmallows

Directions:

1. Put pecans in a single layer on baking sheet.
2. Toast at 350 degrees for 8 minutes.
3. Microwave 1 c butter and semi-sweet chocolate chips in large glass bowl at high for 1 minute or until smooth and completely melted. Stir at 30 second intervals.
4. Whisk sugar and next 5 ingredients into chocolate mixture.
5. Pour the batter into a greased 15x10x1 jelly roll pan.
6. Bake at 350 degrees for 20 minutes.
7. Remove from oven & sprinkle evenly with marshmallows.
8. Bake another 8-10 minutes until golden brown.
9. Drizzle the warm cake with chocolate frosting (softened) and sprinkle with toasted pecans.
10. Cut into small squares and serve.

Blueberry Buckle with Cinnamon-Bourbon Sauce

Contributed by: Deanna Morrell

Directions:

1. Preheat oven 350 degrees.
2. Butter and flour 8" square pan.
3. Using mixture 1 c of butter and 1/3 c sugar until fluffy.
4. Beat in egg.
5. Sift 2 cups flour and baking soda.
6. Stir dry ingredients and buttermilk alternatively into creamed mixture.
7. Spread batter into pan.
8. Cover with berries.
9. Mix next 7 ingredients until crumbly.
10. Sprinkle over berries and bake until top is browned a cake is firm, about 1 hour.

Sauce

1. Melt butter in double boiler over simmering water.
2. Beat sugar, eggs and cinnamon in small bowl, blend well.
3. Stir this mixture into butter. Add hot water and stir until mixture coats the back of a spoon, about 6-8 minutes.
4. Remove from over water.
5. Let cool to room temp.
6. Stir cream and bourbon into sauce.
7. To serve, cut cake into squares.
8. Spoon sauce over cake.

Ingredients:

2 pints of fresh blueberries (add sugar to taste)
2 sticks of softened unsalted butter (room temperature)
1/3 c of sugar
½ c sugar
1 egg, beaten
½ c packed dark brown sugar
2 c flour
½ c chopped toasted pecans
2 tsp baking soda
1 stick of unsalted butter cut into small pieces
1 c buttermilk
½ tsp freshly grated nutmeg
1 c flour
¼ t ground ginger

Sauce

1 stick of unsalted butter
1 Tbsp very hot water
2/3 c of sugar
½ c whipping cream
2 eggs
½ c of bourbon
½ tsp of cinnamon

Everything Cookies

Oatmeal raisin, chocolate chip, molasses cookie all mixed into one

Contributed by: Deanna Morrell

Ingredients:

1 cup (2 sticks) of butter (room temp/softened)
2 c of sugar
2 eggs
1 tbsp. of molasses
2 tsp of vanilla

2 cups of flour
2 tsp of cinnamon
1 ½ tsp of baking soda
½ of salt

2 c of quick oats
⅔ c of raisins
1 c of chopped nuts (optional)
1 c chocolate chips

Directions:

1. Preheat oven to 350 degrees. Cream butter and sugar until smooth. Add eggs one at a time, then molasses and vanilla. Combine flour, cinnamon, soda and salt. Sift together in a separate bowl. Combine last 4 ingredients in a separate bowl. Gradually add flour mixture into creamed mixture. Use a slow to medium mixer speed and mix until smooth. To this mixture add the raisin etc. By hand.

2. Drop rounded teaspoons onto ungreased cookie sheet (works best with silicone mat so they do not stick). Bake 12 minutes or until light brown. The cookies will look a little underdone, so do not overcook. Make sure you keep dough chilled between filling the cookie sheets.

3. Cool 5 minutes and then remove from cookie sheet (they will still be warm). They have a tendency to stick if left too long on the cookie sheet. I like to put the cookies on wax paper and then move them onto the cooling racks so they have a chance to cool completely (about 20 minutes) before you store them. Do not leave them out too long after cooling as they will lose their "chewy" texture and become hard. Store in ziplock bags. Makes about 4 dozen cookies (depending on the size).

Bourbon Applesauce Cake

Contributed by: Deanna Morrell

Directions:

1. Combine ingredients in a large bowl.
2. Beat at medium speed with electric mixer for 3 minutes, scraping down sides of bowl with rubber spatula.
3. Stir in ¾ to 1 c finely chopped walnuts.
4. Pour into 9x5x3 greased & floured loaf pan.
5. Bake 325 degrees for 1½ hours or until center springs back when lightly pressed with finger tips.
6. Cool in pan on wire rack 10 minutes.
7. Loosen around edges with spatula or knife, remove from pan.
8. Cool completely.
9. Sprinkle with 10 X (Confectioners') sugar.
10. Serve with a scoop of your favorite ice cream or whipped cream.
11. Garnish with nuts, cherries, kiwi, etc...your choice (can use candied fruits).

Note: Spoon an additional ¼ cup bourbon or apple cider over cake while it's is still warm if you want.

Ingredients:

½ c (1 stick) butter (room temp/ very soft)
2 eggs (warm, room temp)
1 c firmly packed brown sugar
2 ½ c sifted all-purpose flour
2 tsp baking soda
¼ tsp salt
¼ c wheat germ
2 c sweetened applesauce
¼ c bourbon (apple cider)

Strawberry Trifle Dessert

Contributed by: Linda Miller

Ingredients:

1 Angel Food Cake
1 large pkg of Instant Vanilla pudding
1 quart of fresh strawberries (washed and cut up)
1 large Cool whip

Directions:

1. Tear pieces of the Angel Food Cake and line the bottom of the Trifle bowl
2. Prepare the pudding as directed and spoon on top layer of cake
3. Layer cut strawberries then spoon the cool whip over strawberries
4. Repeat layers ending with cool whip
5. Garnish with a few strawberries
6. Refrigerate until serving

*Can also have a layer of blueberries for a patriotic trifle.

Beverages

What could be better than a great beverage to compliment your dish? Check out these options.

Cappuccino Punch

Contributed by: Heather Abramo

Ingredients:

½ cup instant decaf coffee
1 cup sugar
2 cups hot water
½ gallon Blue Bell vanilla ice cream
½ gallon Blue Bell chocolate ice cream
1 gallon 2% milk
Whipped cream
Nutmeg

Directions:

1. Mix coffee and sugar into 2 cups hot water.
2. Boil until coffee and sugar dissolves.
3. Set aside to cool.
4. Put the ice cream in a large punch bowl.
5. Pour cooled coffee mixture over the ice cream.
6. Add milk.
7. Stir ingredients.
8. Top with whip cream and/or freshly ground nutmeg

Scandinavian Glugg

Holiday Spiced Wine

Contributed by: Jill Van Nuis

Directions:

1. Combine wine, vermouth, sugar, raisins, cardamom, cloves, cinnamon and orange peel.
2. Bring to a boil and reduce heat and simmer for 15 min.
3. Let stand for 12 hours.
4. Before serving, reheat and add vodka and almonds.

Ingredients:

3 quarts dry red wine
1 pint sweet vermouth
1 cup sugar
1 cup raisins
8 whole cardamom – crushed
10 whole cloves
1 stick cinnamon
1 peel orange
1 quart vodka
2 cups blanched almonds

The story ...

This is a recipe passed down from a family ancestor from Norway. Our family makes it every year in December and we serve it throughout the holiday season in festive red mugs. The fantastic smell permeates the air as it simmers on the stove. My kids came home from school one year as it was cooking and announced "It smells like Christmas!" As they've grown, my kids have begun to join in the tradition of celebrating the holidays with this incredible wine that warms your soul, and I have no doubt they will each be serving this to their own families during the Christmas season.

Mai Tai - Kona Version

Contributed by: Deanna Morrell

Ingredients:

2 oz of coconut rum
1 oz of Triple Sec
3pz of Pineapple juice
2 oz of Orange juice
1 oz of Dark Rum

Directions:

1. Combine everything except dark Rum and shake with crushed ice.
2. Wait until shaker has a good frost on the outside before pouring into a DOF glass.
3. Float the dark Rum on top – do not stir.
4. Serve with a pineapple wedge and umbrella.

Chocolate Martini

Contributed by: Deanna Morrell

Directions:

1. Drizzle chocolate syrup down the inside of a martini glass and put in the freezer for 20 minutes or until the drizzle is hard.
2. Mix Martini – 3 oz of Godiva dark chocolate liqueur and 1½ oz of vodka
3. Remove glass from freezer & coat rim with cocoa powder - dip in dark chocolate liqueur and then dip into the cocoa to coat the rim.
4. Place a dark chocolate Hersey's Kiss in the bottom of the glass, then pour in drink.
5. If using a large martini glass, double the drink amount.

Ingredients:

3 oz of Godiva dark chocolate liqueur
½ oz of vodka
chocolate syrup
cocoa powder
Hershey's Kisses

Appendix

This is where we put lots of helpful information, so don't forget these pages!

Cooking Equivalents

3 teaspoons = 1 tablespoon
4 tablespoons = 1/4 cup
5 tablespoons + 1 teaspoon = 1/3 cup
8 tablespoons = 1/2 cup
1 cup = 1/2 pint
2 cups = 1 pint
4 cups (2 pints) = 1 quart
4 quarts = 1 gallon
16 ounces = 1 pound
Dash or pinch = less than 1/8 teaspoon

Common Abbreviations

t	teaspoon
tsp	teaspoon
T	tablespoon
Tbsp	tablespoon
c	cup
oz	ounce
pt	pint
qt	quart
gal	gallon
lb	pound
#	pound

Contributors